American Trailblazers

W9-BSK-749

50

American Trailblazers

50

REMARKABLE PEOPLE
WHO SHAPED U.S. HISTORY

LISA TRUSIANI

ILLUSTRATIONS BY
PAU MORGAN, TOBY NEWSOME, AND CECILIA PUGLESI

ROCKRIDGE
PRESS

Copyright © 2019 by Rockridge Press, Emeryville, California

No part of this publication may be reproduced, stored in a retrieval system or transmitted in any form or by any means, electronic, mechanical, photocopying, recording, scanning or otherwise, except as permitted under Sections 107 or 108 of the 1976 United States Copyright Act, without the prior written permission of the Publisher. Requests to the Publisher for permission should be addressed to the Permissions Department, Rockridge Press, 6005 Shellmound Street, Suite 175, Emeryville, CA 94608.

Limit of Liability/Disclaimer of Warranty: The Publisher and the author make no representations or warranties with respect to the accuracy or completeness of the contents of this work and specifically disclaim all warranties, including without limitation warranties of fitness for a particular purpose. No warranty may be created or extended by sales or promotional materials. The advice and strategies contained herein may not be suitable for every situation. This work is sold with the understanding that the publisher is not engaged in rendering medical, legal, or other professional advice or services. If professional assistance is required, the services of a competent professional person should be sought. Neither the Publisher nor the author shall be liable for damages arising herefrom. The fact that an individual, organization or website is referred to in this work as a citation and/or potential source of further information does not mean that the author or the Publisher endorses the information the individual, organization or website may provide or recommendations they/it may make. Further, readers should be aware that Internet websites listed in this work may have changed or disappeared between when this work was written and when it is read.

For general information on our other products and services or to obtain technical support, please contact our Customer Care Department within the U.S. at (866) 744-2665, or outside the U.S. at (510) 253-0500.

Rockridge Press publishes its books in a variety of electronic and print formats. Some content that appears in print may not be available in electronic books, and vice versa.

TRADEMARKS: Rockridge Press and the Rockridge Press logo are trademarks or registered trademarks of Callisto Media Inc. and/or its affiliates, in the United States and other countries, and may not be used without written permission. All other trademarks are the property of their respective owners. Rockridge Press is not associated with any product or vendor mentioned in this book.

Interior and Cover Designer: Peatra Jariya
Art Manager: Sue Smith
Editor: Mary Colgan
Production Editor: Ashley Polikoff
Illustrations © Kevin Smart/iStock, pp. vi-vii and cover; © 2019 Pau Morgan/Illozoo, pp. viii-ix, 4-7, 20-23, 52-55, 56-59, 80-83, 88-91, 92-95, 96-99, 104-107, 124-127, 132-135, 152-155, 160-163, 168-171, 172-175, 176-179, 192-195, 196-199, 200-203, and cover; © 2019 Toby Newsome/Illozoo, pp. 12-15, 28-31, 32-35, 40-43, 60-63, 72-75, 76-79, 100-103, 108-111, 112-115, 116-119, 120-123, 144-147, 156-159, 184-187 and cover; © 2019 Cecilia Puglesi, pp. x-3, 8-11, 16-19, 24-27, 36-39, 44-47, 48-51, 64-67, 68-71, 84-87, 128-131, 136-139, 140-143, 148-151,164-167, 180-183, 188-191, and cover.

ISBN: Print 978-1-64152-638-8 | eBook 978-1-64152-639-5

This book is dedicated to my children, Grant Parker and Grayson Parker; my husband, Rick Parker; and my parents, Annamarie Ross Trusiani and Paul J. Trusiani. Whether they lead, follow, or walk shoulder-to-shoulder, their presence on the trail gives me hope and inspiration.

Contents

The Stories of 50 Americans

INTRODUCTION

HERE ARE THE STORIES OF 50 AMERICANS.
They differ from each other in race, ethnicity, gender, sexual orientation, education, and socioeconomic status. Some died before they were 40 years old, while others lived into their 90s. Some were born in the 18th century, others in the 20th. Whether they were educated or illiterate, enslaved or free, immigrants or native-born, rich or poor, physically strong or chronically weak, they are all remarkable.

As you read these brief biographies, do you notice a trait or two these people seem to have in common? You may wonder how a person creates art that changes the very idea of art. Or what empowers a person to demand her constitutional rights when doing so means she must defy authorities who are willing to kill or injure her. In these biographies, you will find answers, and you may have many more questions you wish you could ask these people. Some are living, so you can write to them. Most are not, but their work lives on, ready to provide answers to your questions. Each of these individuals made great contributions, not by accident, but through passionate effort.

Charles Samuel Addams

Cartoonist

January 7, 1912–September 29, 1988

Charles "Charlie" Samuel Addams was born in Westfield, New Jersey, a town less than 25 miles from New York City. His mother was a homemaker, and his father was a business executive. As a child, Charles enjoyed playfully scaring his grandmother, who lived with them. He also had a talent for drawing, which his family encouraged, and his cartoons were published in his high school newspaper. He attended universities out of state for a few years, and then he went to art school in New York City. Shortly after Charles enrolled in art school, one of his cartoons was published in *The New Yorker* magazine, which was—and still is—one of the most prestigious magazines for cartoonists.

Charles became one of the most famous cartoonists in the United States, and his popularity continues to this day. Charles was pioneering in his style of humor. It was dark. His morbid cartoons were original and new. *The New Yorker* magazine, which also featured literary fiction, essays, and poetry, published Charles's cartoons for 50 years. Other cartoonists, writers, and comedians continue to be influenced by his work.

Charles created the Addams Family, fictional characters who lived together in a Victorian mansion. Their home looked like the houses Charles saw growing up in Westfield—except the Addams Family house was in a state of decay, making it a perfect home for this household of darkly charming characters. The head of the family is Morticia, a tall, thin, elegant woman, who towers over her adoring husband in a long, slinky, gothic, black evening dress. The character of her husband, Gomez, with a pencil-thin mustache and dark, shiny hair was based on the governor of New York at the time. Pugsley and Wednesday are their beloved children, and Grandmama, Uncle Fester, and Cousin Itt round out this the close-knit, wacky family. Servants include a disembodied hand named Thing and Lurch the Butler. Addams Family cartoons first appeared in *The New Yorker* in 1938. These characters were not named in the cartoons, but they were well defined later in television series, movies, animations, and musical theater. The Addams Family represents the typical American family, while also turning the idea of the typical American family upside down.

"NORMAL IS AN ILLUSION.
WHAT IS NORMAL
FOR THE SPIDER
IS CHAOS
FOR THE FLY."

TIPS FOR YOU!

Sixteen collections of Charles's cartoons have been published and are fun to look at. Find out if your library has one of them. If you like to draw, look at the people around you and turn some of them into cartoon characters.

Louisa May Alcott

ACTIVIST, WRITER

November 29, 1832–March 6, 1888

Louisa May Alcott was born in Germantown, Pennsylvania, and raised near Boston, Massachusetts, with her mother, father, and three sisters. Her mother was active in abolitionist and women's rights movements. She was from an important New England family, whose most famous member was President John Quincy Adams. Louisa's father was a penniless, yet well-known philosopher, educator, and author. His brilliant ideas were often completely impractical. He believed animals on farms shouldn't be used to plow fields or fertilize crops. As a result, his farming community failed within eight months due to food shortages. The Alcott family moved nearly 30 times in 30 years.

Louisa is the author of one of America's best-loved novels, *Little Women*. Like the character Jo in *Little Women*, Louisa had a passion for writing and became a writer to make money. When a publisher asked her to write a story about girls, she said no because she did not think it would be interesting to do and did not believe it would make money. But the publisher promised to publish her father's philosophy book if Louisa wrote a book about girls, so eventually she agreed. She wrote *Little Women* as a favor to her father.

Little Women is about the March family, and each character is based on a member of Louisa's own family. The book was an immediate success, and it is still phenomenally popular today. Louisa used her profits from the book to pay off her family's debts, and they lived comfortably from then on. She wrote many more books after *Little Women*.

People connect to the characters Louisa created in her stories. Most of her books were fiction, but they were influenced by the times she lived in and her family's beliefs. Louisa's family was active in the fight for equality. They hid people who had escaped slavery in the home where Louisa lived and wrote and set the story of *Little Women*. During the Civil War, Louisa sewed uniforms for Union soldiers and worked at a hospital in Washington, DC. She fought for women to have the right to vote. She was also the first woman to register to vote in Concord, Massachusetts.

"... MY GREATEST PRIDE IS IN THE FACT THAT I HAVE LIVED TO KNOW THE BRAVE MEN AND WOMEN WHO DID SO MUCH FOR THE CAUSE (ENDING SLAVERY) ..."

TIPS FOR YOU!

The house Louisa and her family lived in is now a museum called the Orchard House. Take a tour if you can. It's like walking through the Marches' house in *Little Women*. You can also visit the museum online at Louisamayalcott.org.

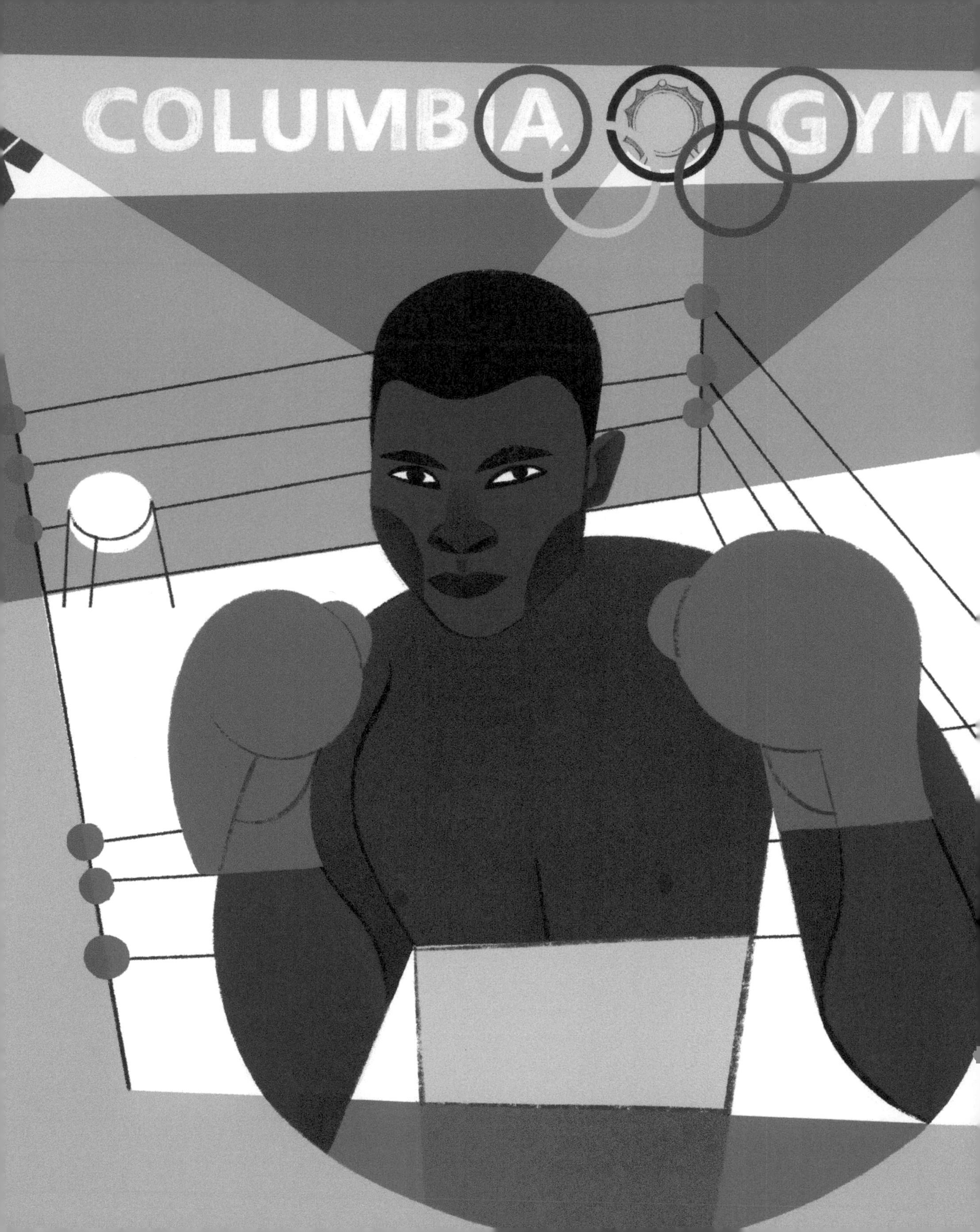
COLUMBIA GYM

Muhammad Ali

ACTIVIST, BOXER

January 17, 1942–June 3, 2016

uhammad Ali was born Cassius Marcellus Clay, Jr. in Louisville, Kentucky. His father was a sign painter, and his mother was a domestic worker. When Cassius was growing up, his city was seg-regated, which means that people were separated based on race. Drinking fountains and restrooms were for "Whites Only" or "Coloreds Only." The boxing gymnasiums where boys and young men trained were also segregated, except for one gym. The Columbia Gym, operated by police officer Joe Martin, was integrated. Whites and blacks trained there together.

Cassius was 12 years old when he rode his new, red, $60 bike to a kids' event downtown. When he discovered his bike had been stolen, he ran into the gym to tell Officer Martin. Cassius said if he found the thief, he would punch him. Martin invited Cassius to come to the gym to learn how to fight. Cassius trained as a boxer, and by the age of 18, he had won the overwhelming majority of his amateur boxing matches. He wanted to box professionally, but Martin convinced him to compete in the Olympics first. He won a gold medal in the 1960 Olympic games in Rome and wore his medal day and night. When he returned to the United States, countless managers and trainers wanted to sponsor his professional career.

In the next few years, Cassius stunned the world by beating heavy-weight champion Sonny Liston. He also converted to the religion of Islam and changed his name to Muhammad Ali. Cassius—now Muhammad—successfully defended his championship title with quick victories. In 1967, he refused to report to a military base to be inducted into the U.S. military during the Vietnam War. He was arrested for evading the draft, convicted, sentenced to a prison term of five years, and fined $10,000. His championship boxing titles were taken from him. He was not allowed to compete in boxing in the U.S. for three years and was not allowed to leave the U.S. He appealed the conviction, and the U.S. Supreme Court overturned it. Although he did not go to prison while his case was being appealed, he was unable to make a living as a boxer. He was stripped of his sense of self and his identity for four years. Then his boxing career continued. By the time he retired in 1981, his record was 56 wins and 5 losses. He was the only boxer to win the heavyweight championship title three times.

Muhammad enjoyed getting media attention for his boxing matches. In the weeks before a match, he teased his opponents and promoted him-self with colorful rhymes. Here is a favorite: "Float like a butterfly, sting like a bee. The hands can't hit what the eyes can't see."

"I AM AMERICA. I AM THE PART YOU WON'T RECOGNIZE. BUT GET USED TO ME—BLACK, CONFIDENT, COCKY; MY NAME, NOT YOURS; MY RELIGION, NOT YOURS; MY GOALS, MY OWN. GET USED TO ME."

TIPS FOR YOU!

Muhammad Ali wrote the book *Healing* to teach tolerance. To learn more about his charity work, efforts to promote peace, and many national and international awards, visit the Muhammad Ali Center in Lexington, Kentucky, or read about it online at Alicenter.org.

John James Audubon

ARTIST, CONSERVATIONIST, ORNITHOLOGIST

April 26, 1785–January 27, 1851

John James Audubon was born Jean Rabine in Saint-Domingue, which is now Haiti. He and a half-sibling were raised by their father in France, where John spent countless hours observing birds and drawing. By age 18, he was a skilled marksman, fencer, horseman, and musician. To avoid being forced to serve in Napoleon Bonaparte's army, John was sent to the United States, where his father had a farm and mill, called Mill Grove. Young Audubon was lucky he landed where he did. He met a neighbor's daughter, Lucy, and they were soon married.

While at Mill Grove, John observed where birds lived and how they behaved. He would shoot a specimen, pose it, and then illustrate it. Instead of a black background, which was typical at the time, he set the bird in a realistic scene. John had an idea that birds returned to the nest where they were hatched. To test his theory, he tied a string around the legs of fledglings. A year or two later, the birds did return. This method of "banding" birds to track them is now a routine part of ornithology, or the study of birds.

John and Lucy eventually sold Mill Grove and moved to Kentucky to begin a new life. Lucy worked to support herself and their children, while John traveled around North America observing and painting birds. After he had finished hundreds of life-size paintings, he brought them to England to try to get them published in a book. The Royal Institution of Liverpool, England, exhibited his remarkable work. The response was overwhelmingly enthusiastic, and he received the funding he needed. In fact, John became a celebrity. A printer agreed to create etchings of the paintings, which were needed to print the book. After John spent several years traveling back and forth between England and the U.S., the printer finished a giant book, titled *The Birds of America*. Only 90 copies were made, and the price was $100 per book the year it was published. Since few books remain intact today, they are worth about $10 million each. John went on to publish many other successful nature books, travel books, and observation journals.

Fifty-four years after John's death, conservationists created The National Audubon Society to protect birds and their habitats. It remains strong today. His paintings and etchings are on display in numerous museums. These masterpieces are considered important contributions to both science and art.

"A TRUE CONSERVATIONIST IS A MAN WHO KNOWS THAT THE WORLD IS NOT GIVEN BY HIS FATHERS, BUT BORROWED FROM HIS CHILDREN."

TIPS FOR YOU!

You can visit the National Audubon Society online to learn more about birds, the work the organization does, and the person who inspired them. Go to Audubon.org.

Josephine Baker

SINGER, ACTIVIST, WWII FRENCH RESISTANCE AGENT

June 3, 1906—April 12, 1975

Josephine Baker was born Freda Josephine McDonald in St. Louis, Missouri. She grew up in two worlds: traveling with her parents, who were entertainers in the Midwest, and working in white people's homes washing laundry and babysitting. The two worlds had something in common: They were both segregated based on skin color. At the age of 15, Josephine ran away with a group of entertainers and married a man named Willie Baker. She took his name and kept it after they divorced and even after she remarried and divorced several more times.

Right from the start, Josephine showed immense talent as a singer and dancer. Audiences also loved how funny she was. In New York, she performed in Harlem nightclubs and became part of the explosion of black culture known as the Harlem Renaissance. A producer, who saw her in the U.S., invited her to Paris to perform in an all-black review that combined singing, dancing, and short comedy routines. While performing in the capital of France, Josephine discovered life was very different from U.S. cities. In Paris, people were not segregated, or separated by race. The city was integrated, and Josephine was respected and adored. She became a star. She made a fortune. When the Nazis occupied Paris, Josephine continued her career on stage, often performing for Nazis. They were unaware that off-stage, Josephine worked with the French Resistance, helping refugees escape and using invisible ink on her sheet music to sneak messages past the Nazis to other agents in the Resistance. After the war, the French government awarded Josephine medals and named her a Chevalier of the Legion of Honor. *Chevalier* means "knight" in French.

Josephine's career included multiple tours in the United States. In 1936, the U.S. press scorned her, calling her a "negro wench." She returned to France, heartbroken by this rejection. After World War II, she came back to the U.S. for concert tours, and she refused to perform for segregated audiences. In the 1950s and 1960s, Josephine joined the civil rights movement in the U.S. For instance, she participated in the March on Washington with Martin Luther King Jr. in 1963. Her efforts, like those of many others, helped defeat segregation laws in the U.S. Ten years later, Josephine received a standing ovation at Carnegie Hall in New York City, one of the most famous concert halls in the nation. The entire audience was on its feet, applauding her as she walked across the stage to begin her first song. She was so touched, she burst into tears. What followed was one of her characteristically phenomenal performances.

"YOU KNOW, FRIENDS, THAT I DO NOT LIE TO YOU WHEN I TELL YOU I HAVE WALKED INTO THE PALACES OF KINGS AND QUEENS AND INTO THE HOUSES OF PRESIDENTS. AND MUCH MORE. BUT I COULD NOT WALK INTO A HOTEL IN AMERICA AND GET A CUP OF COFFEE, AND THAT MADE ME MAD."

TIPS FOR YOU!

You can make invisible ink by mixing lemon and equal amounts of baking soda and water. Dip a clean, thin brush or cotton swab into the mixture and write your message on a white piece of paper. Let the paper dry completely, then wipe it with a small amount of dark grape juice to reveal the message.

S. Stillman Berry

MARINE ZOOLOGIST

March 16, 1887–April 9, 1984

Samuel Stillman Berry was born in Unity, Maine, when his mother was visiting relatives. His parents were natives of Maine who had moved to Montana in 1880 and owned a 50,000-acre sheep ranch. However, Stillman was unable to live in Montana because of his frail health. His mother moved with him to many different places, including the southwest because of its dry, arid climate. He was an only child, but his mother was also raising her nieces, so he had their company throughout most of his childhood. When Stillman was 11 years old, he moved with his family to Redlands, California. Except for time away at college, Redlands was Stillman's home for the rest of his 97 years.

Stillman was a gentleman scientist, which means he was a wealthy man who was a scientist because he liked the work and did not need to be paid. He created and controlled his own scientific research projects and paid for them with income from his family's ranch. He attended Stanford University, earning a degree in zoology, then went to Harvard University for his master's degree. He returned to Stanford to study ocean animals and earned a PhD in marine zoology. Stillman's PhD thesis is, to this day, one of the most important studies of cephalopods (a type of mollusk) found in the Pacific Ocean.

Stillman was a brilliant man who knew a great deal about a great many things. As a scientist, his area of greatest knowledge was mollusks, which made him a malacologist. What's a mollusk? Mollusks include squids and octopuses, but also mussels, slugs, and snails. These animals have soft bodies and live in water or wet places. They are invertebrates, which means they do not have a backbone, but most have a shell. Stillman knew mollusks inside and out. He collected them, studied them in laboratories, drew pictures of them, and wrote scientific articles about them. Sometimes he figured out that the little shelled creature he was holding in his hand had never been discovered by a scientist before, and he introduced it to the scientific world.

Over his career, Stillman published more than 200 scientific articles on marine mollusks and land snails. Twenty-eight kinds of mollusks are named after him.

"THE CAMP STOVES HAD BEEN SET UP AND THE GRUB WAS COOKING, ALONG BOOMED A DREADFULLY BLACK AND DARK CLOUD AND IT BEGAN TO HAIL—STONES THE SIZE OF PIGEON EGGS AT FIRST, BUT GRADUALLY GETTING SMALLER UNTIL TOWARD THE END THEY WERE ONLY SIZE OF BUCKSHOT."

FROM A CHILDHOOD LETTER TO HIS MOTHER WHILE HE WAS WITH A GROUP ON THE RANGE, TAKING CARE OF SHEEP

TIPS FOR YOU!

Imagine being the first person to discover a kind of plant or animal. What would you like to discover? What would you name it?

Alexander Calder

SCULPTOR

August 22, 1898–November 11, 1976

Alexander "Sandy" Calder was born in Lawnton, Pennsylvania. His mother was a portrait painter, and his father was a sculptor. They encouraged Sandy and his sister to create art, and Sandy liked to use wire, string, metal foil, and fabric to build figures. After high school, Sandy earned a degree in engineering and worked for four years before moving to New York City to study art.

Sandy became one of the greatest innovators in modern art. Like his father and his father's father, he created large artworks for public spaces. His grandfather created the William Penn statue that is on top of City Hall in Philadelphia. His father's sculpture of George Washington is part of the Washington Square Arch in New York City. Unlike his family's artwork, Sandy's public sculptures were not of historic figures. He made simple shapes out of industrial materials like steel and aluminum and then placed them together. The space in between the solid forms is as important as the forms themselves. Hundreds of his massive abstract sculptures are on permanent display around the world.

Throughout most of his career, Sandy built stationary statues. Like most sculptures, they were motionless. Starting in 1931, he created a new kind of art, called "mobiles." These sculptures moved. At first, he used machines to make his sculptures move, but soon he began to use air currents. He created sculptures that floated in the air, usually suspended from a ceiling. These sculptures can appear alive to viewers. They are always moving, always responding to breezes, no matter how small. Little ripples of air created when a door opens, a child runs, or a person breathes move mobiles. The ever-changing air currents create "drawings in space." In the United States and in countries around the world, Sandy was—and is—treasured, and his original artworks are considered masterpieces.

"TO MOST PEOPLE WHO LOOK AT A MOBILE, IT'S NO MORE THAN A SERIES OF FLAT OBJECTS THAT MOVE. TO A FEW, IT MAY BE POETRY."

TIPS FOR YOU!

Abstract artists use line, color, and form to create art. Sandy found a way to use movement as well. Create your own hanging sculpture, or mobile. Use a wire hanger, strings, and paper. Make it any way you want. Have fun. Sandy did.

Rachel Carson

Ecologist, Scientist, Writer

May 27, 1907–April 14, 1964

Rachel Louise Carson was born in Springdale, Pennsylvania, a rural area along the Allegheny River. As a child, she loved reading, writing, and spending time outside surrounded by nature. She earned a college degree in biology and then went to Johns Hopkins University, where she received a master's in zoology. Rachel wrote newspaper articles about nature and worked as a marine biologist for the U.S. Fish and Wildlife Service.

Rachel wrote books that captured both the science and the wonder of the natural world. Her classic, *The Sea Around Us*, was published in 1951. It was an instant bestseller and won the National Book Award for nonfiction. Her most famous book is *Silent Spring*. This book sounded the alarm about pollution's terrible effects on the environment. Rachel warned that a popular pesticide, DDT, was unlike any other pesticide used before. It didn't only kill the insects people wanted dead; it killed or damaged every living thing in its path. DDT polluted the air, water, and soil. It killed birds and fish. It poisoned the plants people ate and stayed in people's bodies. Rachel's warning angered the chemical industry that made and sold DDT. The agricultural industry wanted to keep spraying it on plants. The government wanted to use it, too. But people wanted answers from the government. Rachel was invited to testify before Congress. In 1963, she demanded that Congress pass laws to protect both the environment and human health. Approximately 10 years later, DDT was banned for agricultural use in the United States.

Silent Spring did more than warn about the dangers of pollution. It urged people to act. It challenged assumptions about the relationship between humans and the environment. Rachel did not accept the idea that it was wise for humans to control nature or that it was even possible. She showed that trying to dominate nature threw the ecosystem out of balance and that people could be harmed by this imbalance. *Silent Spring* motivated people to question authorities, like scientists, corporations, and the government. It formed the basis for a new area of study called conservation. And it helped create the environmental movement that is still fighting to protect the Earth today.

"IF THERE IS POETRY IN MY BOOK ABOUT THE SEA, IT IS NOT BECAUSE I DELIBERATELY PUT IT THERE, BUT BECAUSE NO ONE COULD WRITE TRUTHFULLY ABOUT THE SEA AND LEAVE OUT THE POETRY."

TIPS FOR YOU!

Rachel wanted people to look at how they lived their lives and try to make a smaller impact on the environment. Can you think of ways to reduce, reuse, and recycle?

Shirley Chisholm

U.S. REPRESENTATIVE FROM NEW YORK, PRESIDENTIAL CANDIDATE, ACTIVIST

November 30, 1924–January 1, 2005

Shirley Anita St. Hill Chisholm was born in Brooklyn, New York. Her parents were from Guyana and Barbados, and they sent Shirley and her sister to Barbados to live part time with relatives on the family's farm. She earned a full scholarship to Brooklyn College, where she did well academically and excelled in debate competitions. When a whites-only social club refused to let her and other nonwhite students join, Shirley started her own club. After college, she worked as a preschool teacher and then a daycare director. She consulted with the New York City government about the welfare of children and became an expert in early education. She was also very involved in her community.

Shirley ran for office when a new congressional district was created in Brooklyn. She beat three well-qualified challengers in the Democratic primary, and then defeated a Republican in the general election. Her opponent held the same liberal positions Shirley did and had impressive qualifications as a civil rights activist. However, he also believed that women had already become too powerful in politics. This sexist attitude made him less popular as a candidate, though he was also a Republican in an overwhelmingly Democratic district.

By winning this election, Shirley became the first African American woman in Congress. It didn't take long for Shirley's colleagues in the House of Representatives to get to know her. She spoke out immediately, giving powerful speeches on the House floor. She opposed the Vietnam War. She pushed for policies to help working people and the poor, and noted they are often the same people. She fought for increased educational funding. Shirley won six reelections and served as a representative from 1969 to 1983. She fought to be on important committees in the House, so that the people she represented had a voice in decisions about education, labor, political reforms, and the economy. Other Democrats criticized Shirley for working with Republicans, as some had extreme views on race. But she felt it was important to compromise and "build bridges between communities" to push legislation forward.

Shirley helped found the Congressional Black Caucus in 1971 and the Congressional Women's Caucus in 1977. She ran for president of the United States in 1972 but did not receive enough votes in the primary to become the Democratic nominee. Even so, her national campaign for president accomplished Shirley's goal, which was to bring attention to gender discrimination and racism.

"LADIES AND GENTLEMEN . . .
THIS IS FIGHTING
SHIRLEY CHISHOLM
COMING THROUGH."

TIPS FOR YOU!

Shirley used her voice to create change. You can learn more about her and other leaders in black history by reading *Young, Gifted, and Black: Meet 52 Black Heroes from Past and Present* by Jamia Wilson.

Roberto Clemente

BASEBALL LEGEND, ACTIVIST

August 18, 1934–December 31, 1972

Roberto Enrique Clemente Walker was born in Puerto Rico, which means he was a U.S. citizen. The youngest of seven children, Roberto grew up playing on a neighborhood baseball team against other local teams. He loved it, and he wasn't alone in his love for the sport. Baseball was, and is, the most popular sport in Puerto Rico. When Roberto played, the games could last all day, and he might hit as many as 10 home runs. He also excelled at the high jump and the javelin throw. But rather than train for the Olympics in these sports, he decided to pursue professional baseball.

Roberto went to a tryout camp for professional baseball, and scouts from both island and mainland baseball teams were impressed by him. He was quickly signed by a professional team in Puerto Rico and played on the team for several seasons. This team also had great Negro league baseball players managing and playing on the team.

The Negro leagues were any of the groups of baseball teams with all nonwhite players in the U.S. during the time that major and minor league baseball in the U.S. was segregated. These island and Negro league managers and players helped develop Roberto into an even more skillful player. In 1954, the Brooklyn Dodgers signed Roberto and sent him to play on their best minor league team. After the 1954 season, another major league team, the Pittsburgh Pirates, picked Roberto.

Roberto played for the Pirates for 18 years. At the beginning, he faced some challenges. He was one of the first nonwhite players on the team, since the Pirates had stopped excluding people of color only the year before and Roberto was one of the team's first players from Puerto Rico. Plus, Roberto did not know English yet and needed to rely on bilingual teammates to help him. In 1960, Roberto had a great season and helped the Pirates beat the New York Yankees for the World Series title. He continued to excel for the rest of his career. He was the National League batting champion four times, won the 1966 National League Most Valuable Player award, received 12 Gold Glove awards, and nabbed the Most Valuable Player award for his role in the Pirates winning the World Series again in 1971. He is also one of the few players to be a member of Major League Baseball's 3000 Hit Club, which means he had at least 3,000 hits during the regular seasons of his major league career. In 1973, he became the first player born in Latin America to be voted into the Baseball Hall of Fame.

When Roberto was not playing baseball, he spent time with his family and did charity work. On December 31, 1972, Roberto was taking supplies to earthquake victims in Nicaragua. Tragically, the plane crashed, and there were no survivors. On April 6, 1973, Roberto's uniform number, 21, was retired by the Pirates in his honor.

"ANY TIME YOU HAVE AN OPPOR-
TUNITY TO MAKE A DIFFERENCE
IN THIS WORLD AND YOU DON'T,
THEN YOU ARE WASTING YOUR
TIME ON EARTH."

TIPS FOR YOU!

Be like Roberto and volunteer.
Find out if your school has an
organization that helps people
and sign up to make a difference in
this world.

CLAUDETTE COLVIN

CIVIL RIGHTS ACTIVIST, NURSE'S AIDE

September 5, 1939–

Claudette Colvin was born in Montgomery, Alabama. She was adopted by an aunt and uncle, who gave her love and security while raising her in the poorest section of Montgomery. They lived in a black-only neighborhood, and Claudette attended a black-only school, where she earned good grades. She also joined a civil rights group for students and learned about the equal rights that the U.S. Constitution guarantees to all United States citizens.

Claudette is a pioneer in the civil rights movement. Her intelligence and bravery helped bring an end to segregation laws in the South that kept whites and blacks separate in neighborhoods, schools, swimming pools, movie theaters, public restrooms, and restaurants. These rules, called Jim Crow laws, also meant that black people had to give up their seats to white people on public buses. But on March 2, 1955, when she was just 15 years old, Claudette said *no*.

The bus driver told her to give her seat to a white passenger, but she refused. The police arrived and demanded that she give up her seat, but she did not. They put her in handcuffs, arrested her, and roughly took her off the bus. After Claudette had spent three hours in jail, her minister paid her bail and Claudette went home.

Later that year, Rosa Parks refused to give up her seat to a white passenger. Like Claudette, she was arrested. Unlike Claudette, Rosa was an adult, which was one reason African American leaders decided to publicize her arrest and ask black citizens to protest by not riding city buses. This was the beginning of the Montgomery bus boycott. Rosa Parks is more famous for her role in ending segregation on buses, but other brave people, like Claudette, played important parts, too.

In 1956, Claudette and three other women went to court. Their lawyers argued Montgomery's public bus laws were unconstitutional because the U.S. Constitution guarantees equal treatment to U.S. citizens of any race. The U.S. Supreme Court agreed. The city was no longer allowed to force black people to give up their seats to whites. After new laws went into effect in Montgomery, blacks began riding the buses again. The boycott had lasted 381 days. Its success inspired people across the country to challenge laws that discriminated against people of color. Within 10 years, most Jim Crow laws had been ruled unconstitutional.

"THE SPIRIT OF
HARRIET TUBMAN AND
SOJOURNER TRUTH WAS IN ME.
I DIDN'T GET UP."

TIPS FOR YOU!

When the police arrested Claudette, she lifted her voice and told people around her that this treatment was unconstitutional. She knew her civil rights, and you can learn about your civil rights, too. Visit the American Civil Liberties Union at Aclu.org.

Elizabeth Sprague Coolidge

COMPOSER, PIANIST, PATRON OF THE ARTS

October 30, 1864–November 4, 1953

Elizabeth "Liz" Sprague Coolidge was born in Chicago, Illinois. Her father was a wealthy merchant who was a patron of the Chicago Symphony Orchestra. Music was important to the family, and Liz became a talented musician. She studied piano and composition at home with well-respected teachers.

Most wealthy American young women of this time went on a "European tour," and Liz did, too. For nearly a year, she traveled with her parents to the most important concert halls in Europe, listened to world-renowned opera singers and orchestras, and studied the piano with expert music teachers. After her return to the U.S., Liz was devoted to music and collaborated both with other musicians in Chicago and European musicians who were performing in the U.S.

In 1891, Liz married a physician. They moved to Massachusetts, and a few years later had a son. In an era when women were generally subservient to their fathers and then to their husbands, it was unusual that Liz's husband supported her dedication to music, although Liz likely would not have married him if he had not. Liz was busy with music. She composed music and performed piano concerts to raise money for charities. However, this great joy was also a growing frustration as she began to lose her hearing. Over time, her deafness grew more severe, and Liz needed hearing aids to play music, collaborate with musicians, and listen to concerts.

After Liz's husband and parents died, she used much of her inheritance to promote chamber music in the United States. Chamber music is a form of classical music, but it is played by only a few musicians rather than an entire orchestra. For instance, a chamber music trio might be composed of two violinists and a cellist. While chamber music today is admired and respected, in the early twentieth century, it was far less so. Liz made extraordinary contributions to building its popularity. She created a foundation that paid for a new auditorium to be built and provided money for concerts to be held there. She also helped develop the Berkshire Symphonic Festival at Tanglewood, still one of the most important summer music festivals in the country.

Liz commissioned chamber music as well. This means she paid composers to write new music with the idea that it would be played at a special event, such as a festival. Some of the most famous music compositions were commissioned by Liz. One example is "Appalachian Spring" by Aaron Copland. Other composers whose work she supported include Samuel Barber, Maurice Ravel, and Igor Stravinsky.

"I FEEL THAT
THE SURVIVAL
OF THE HUMAN SPIRIT
LARGELY DEPENDS UPON ITS
ARTISTIC FREEDOM."

TIPS FOR YOU!

Chamber music ensembles come in a variety of sizes. How many musicians do you think play in a duet, trio, quartet, quintet, sextet, septet, octet, nonet, and dectet? Can you find any ensembles like these to listen to online?

Joe Medicine Crow

WAR CHIEF, HISTORIAN

October 27, 1913–April 3, 2016

Joseph Medicine Crow (or "High Bird") was born on the Crow Indian Reservation in Montana. His mother was Amy Yellowtail and his father was Leo Medicine Crow. Joe went to school on the reservation as a child and later moved to California to study anthropology at the University of Southern California. He wrote his final thesis on the impact of European culture on the Crow Indian Tribe and was awarded a master's degree.

A few years after graduating from college, Joe joined the U.S. Army during World War II. Like his father, Joe completed the four steps necessary to become a Crow war chief. He did this during his military service, wearing war paint under his uniform. He touched his enemy without killing him. He took his enemy's weapon. He led a group of soldiers to success. He stole the enemy's horse. After the war, Joe returned to the Crow Nation and served as its anthropologist and historian. Being "keeper of memories" was a familiar role.

During childhood, Joe spent countless hours with one of his mother's elderly relatives, White Man Runs Him. He had been a scout for General George A. Custer, commander of the cavalry at the Battle of Little Big Horn on the Crow Indian Reservation in 1876. It was a Crow tradition for history to be passed from one generation to the next through storytelling. When White Man Runs Him told Joe stories about what he had seen with his own eyes at this famous battle where Custer was killed and the U.S. military was defeated, he was not only entertaining a child, but giving pieces of the tribe's history for this child to take into the future.

Joe shared his knowledge and experience in many ways. He wrote books about Native American history and about the Crow Nation, including stories about his own life on the Crow Indian Reservation. He lectured and taught at colleges and museums and appeared in documentaries as the last surviving person to hear firsthand accounts of the 1876 Battle of Little Bighorn. In 2009, Joe was given the Presidential Medal of Freedom by President Barack Obama. It is the highest honor a civilian can be awarded in the United States.

"I WAS NEVER A SMART MAN TO BEGIN WITH, BUT I LOVE TO LEARN. THIS IS THE WAY TO GET SOMEWHERE IN LIFE."

TIPS FOR YOU!

Ask your family members to tell you stories of life when they were children as well as stories they heard from their older relatives. Write them down and commit them to memory. You can become the historian of your family!

CHARLES RICHARD DREW

DOCTOR, MEDICAL RESEARCHER

June 3, 1904–April 1, 1950

Charles Richard Drew was born in Washington, D.C. His parents raised Charles and his younger siblings in a middle-class, integrated neighborhood. After graduating from Amherst College, he taught college classes and then attended McGill University in Canada. He graduated second in his class, earning a medical degree.

Charles was a surgeon who researched methods of storing blood from donors. The blood was then used in transfusions. When a person bleeds a lot from an injury or surgery, the blood loss can be fatal. A blood transfusion replaces that blood and can often save the person's life.

Before 1940, a donor giving blood needed to be next to the patient receiving blood because a tube went directly from the donor's vein to the recipient's. This changed when scientists figured out how to store blood for later use. Charles took this idea a step further by creating bloodmobiles. These specially designed buses were set up with everything needed to draw blood from a donor and store it. Bloodmobiles carried the blood to a facility called a blood bank where it could be kept until needed. The blood was analyzed for type and also screened for germs before being given to a recipient.

Charles was asked to take charge of the Red Cross Blood Bank. It supplied blood to the U.S. military. During World War II, Charles worked to save the lives of soldiers by providing an ample supply of blood. It was well-known that the blood from people of different races was the same, yet African Americans were not allowed to donate blood to help soldiers. After Charles fought to let them be donors, they were. However, the military and state governments ordered blood from whites and blacks to be separated and given only to patients of the same race. Charles resigned from the Red Cross because the military insisted that blood be separated by race. He went on to work as a surgeon and professor of medicine at Howard University. He taught many African Americans to be doctors and surgeons.

During his lifetime, Charles stood up for what he believed in. Today, the American Red Cross Blood Bank stores 40 percent of the nation's blood donations, thanks to the work of Charles Richard Drew.

"THERE IS NO SCIENTIFIC BASIS FOR THE SEPARATION OF THE BLOODS OF DIFFERENT RACES EXCEPT ON THE BASIS OF THE INDIVIDUAL BLOOD TYPES."

TIPS FOR YOU!

There are eight blood types:
A+, A-, B+, B-, O+, O-, AB+, AB-.
Ask your parents what
your blood type is.
Look up the terms *universal donor
and universal recipient*. Is some-
one in your family either?

Sylvia Alice Reade Earle

EXPLORER, MARINE BIOLOGIST, ACTIVIST

August 30, 1935–

Sylvia Alice Reade Earle was born in Gibbstown, New Jersey. At an early age, she moved with her parents to the west coast of Florida and lived on the Gulf of Mexico. Sylvia was always interested in the environment and decided to study natural science in college. She earned degrees in science and then received a PhD in phycology, the study of algae, from Duke University. Sylvia was interested in finding ways to spend more time doing scientific research deep down in the ocean. If only she could live in the sea rather than diving from the surface, it would save so much time when doing underwater research. Around this time, Sylvia learned about the Tektite project.

Tektite was an underwater habitat and laboratory where marine scientists lived and worked for weeks at a time. Two giant capsules, connected by a corridor, were located 50 feet below the surface in a bay in the Virgin Islands. The underwater station was designed for NASA (National Aeronautics and Space Administration) to study how people react to an environment with these extreme physical conditions. In 1970, Sylvia joined the Tektite project and led the first all-women crew to the underwater marine station. The women were *aquanauts*, which means they were both scientists and scuba divers. Sylvia and her team conducted detailed ecological studies in the underwater laboratory. At the same time, NASA studied Sylvia and her team to see how they reacted to being underwater nonstop for weeks, since being underwater is similar to being in outer space. During the two weeks Sylvia spent in the laboratory, she spent 86 hours in the water studying algae.

Over the decades, Sylvia has continued to do important and fascinating work. As an expert in oil spills, she is often called to the scene of a spill to assess the environmental damage. She was the first woman appointed to the position of Chief Scientist at NOAA (National Oceanic and Atmospheric Administration), and she is currently a National Geographic Explorer-in-Residence.

Sylvia has dedicated herself to expanding the field of marine biology, improving the health of the world's oceans, and helping people understand how they are connected to the ocean no matter where in the world they live. She is also a member of Ocean Elders, a worldwide group of activists who work to protect Earth's oceans.

"EVEN IF YOU NEVER HAVE THE CHANCE TO SEE OR TOUCH THE OCEAN, THE OCEAN TOUCHES YOU WITH EVERY BREATH YOU TAKE, EVERY DROP OF WATER YOU DRINK, EVERY BITE YOU CONSUME."

TIPS FOR YOU!

Did you know that every day you breathe oxygen produced by algae? You can learn more about the oceans and Sylvia by watching the documentary *Mission Blue*.

Dian Fossey

PRIMATOLOGIST, ACTIVIST

January 16, 1932–December 26, 1985

Dian Fossey was born in San Francisco, California. She loved animals and became a prize-winning equestrian, or horse rider. Dian was inspired to go to Africa after friends returned from a trip there and showed her their photographs. Dian visited several countries in Africa, and while there she met Mary and Louis Leakey, archaeologists famous for discovering fossils of early humans. She also went to see mountain gorillas in the wild in Uganda. Watching them changed her life. Dian returned to the U.S., but she knew she would go to Africa again. In a fortunate turn of events, Louis Leakey gave a lecture in Kentucky, where Dian lived. Dian attended. When they spoke afterward, Louis invited Dian to study the gorillas in Africa.

Dian went to the Virunga Mountain Range in Uganda and lived in a tent near the gorillas. It took time, but the gorillas habituated to, or grew used to, seeing Dian. At first, she drew pictures of their noses, "noseprints," to tell them apart. Over time, she began to recognize them by their behaviors, too. Dian was forced to leave when fighting among humans broke out nearby. She left Uganda and set up a new camp in Rwanda. At the new camp, called Karisoke, Dian started the process of living near a different group of mountain gorillas. They accepted her more easily when she walked bent over with her hands in fists and her knuckles dragging on the ground. Eventually, Dian was able to recognize individuals by appearance and behavior, and gave them names—like Uncle Bert, named for a relative back in the U.S.

Dian studied the gorillas in the wild for 18 years. She wanted people to know that the critically endangered mountain gorillas were disappearing. One reason was poaching, which means people were killing them illegally. They did this to sell gorilla parts for trophies, food, and traditional medicine. To protect the gorillas from poaching, Dian hired more guards. She also asked the public for help. Previously, the National Geographic Society had visited Dian and photographed the gorillas, so people around the world knew and cared about them. Everyone's favorite was Digit, a young gorilla that Dian loved and had been the first gorilla to accept her. When poachers killed Digit, people around the world were horrified and sent money to help Dian fight the poachers.

In 1983, Dian took a job teaching at a university in the U.S. and wrote the book *Gorillas in the Mist* about her time with the gorillas. Although Dian died tragically in Rwanda in 1985, her conservation work continues through her foundation, the Dian Fossey Gorilla Fund.

"ONE OF THE BASIC STEPS IN SAVING A THREATENED SPECIES IS TO LEARN MORE ABOUT IT."

TIPS FOR YOU!

Many people continue to work to protect the mountain gorillas, and their status has improved from critically endangered to endangered. Today there are about 1,000 in the wild. To learn more about protecting them, visit Gorillafund.org.

Yun Gee

ARTIST, POET

February 22, 1906–June 5, 1963

Yun Gee was born in Canton, China. At the age of 15, he immigrated to the United States, joining his father, a businessman, in San Francisco. While the United States wanted male Asians for cheap, menial labor, there was also intense racism toward Asians. The United States government did not want Asian immigrants to marry each other or to have children together. To prevent this, laws banned Asian women from immigrating to the United States, so Yun's mother was left behind, unable to join her family.

Yun lived in San Francisco's Chinatown, became a U.S. citizen, and attended the California School of Fine Arts (now the San Francisco Art Institute). His paintings were original and bold—even audacious. Yun founded a gallery with some artist friends and began to have art shows. His renown (or popularity as an artist) grew as he moved from San Francisco to Paris to New York, back to Paris, and then to New York again. More people became interested in seeing his work and were eager to see what he would do next. He created oil paintings, watercolors, and sculptures. He also wrote poems and displayed them with his paintings.

Yun's work changed throughout his career, but it was always dynamic and full of energy. It was influenced by politics, literature, and art, and his familiarity with Asia, Europe, and America. Another influence on his work was the absence of his mother, which was a theme he returned to again and again.

Yun's life and work were exciting. He was married to a European princess for a short time. His work was exhibited in famous American museums and in the best galleries in Paris. He married an American and they had a child. Despite the joys in his life and the success in his career, Yun always felt the pain of racism against Asians. Today, his work is respected and in demand. There was a solo exhibit of his work in Taipei, Taiwan, as recently as 2011.

"WHEN I VISITED THE LOUVRE DAY AFTER DAY, THE MASTERPIECES THERE SPOKE TO ME IN A LANGUAGE THAT WAS NEITHER FRENCH NOR CHINESE, BUT WHICH TRANSCENDED TIME AND PLACE."

TIPS FOR YOU!

To learn more about Yun Gee, visit Yungee.com. You will see a photo of him as a child, view his oil paintings and watercolors, read his poetry, and find articles written about him.

George Gershwin

COMPOSER, PIANIST

September 26, 1898–July 11, 1937

George Gershwin was born Jacob Bruskin Gershowitz on the second floor of a tenement building in Brooklyn, New York. It was a world very different from the one his parents had been born into. The Brooklyn neighborhood was filled with Jewish people, just like the places his parents had lived in Russia and Lithuania, but it was America. The United States offered great possibilities for the boatloads of Jewish people fleeing anti-Jewish laws in Eastern Europe.

Coming to America changed the lives of immigrants, but these newcomers and their children changed America, too. They had an impact on everything about the country, including its music. George discovered his passion for music at the age of 10, when his parents bought a secondhand piano, and he started to take lessons. At 15, George dropped out of school and began to make a living playing piano in Tin Pan Alley, a street in New York City where music publishing companies were located. He played the piano for a publisher of sheet music, so people could hear the songs and then buy the sheet music.

George played other people's songs but also started to write his own. He soon became a popular pianist throughout New York City. His fame grew when one of his original songs was featured in a hit play on Broadway. The more music George wrote, the more popular he became across the country and around the world. During his lifetime, George wrote hundreds of songs, including "Rhapsody in Blue," which is perhaps his most famous composition. He often wrote the songs for an entire movie or Broadway musical. His music was the most popular of its time and continues to be loved by musicians, music critics, and people who love singing and listening to music.

George's music was influenced by traditional Jewish songs, American showtunes, jazz and folk songs, and French classical music. He went to Paris and asked famous French classical musicians to teach him, but they refused because they did not want his music to lose its jazz. For some musicians, combining different styles of music can create a mishmash mess. But George was a musical genius who created masterpieces in his original style. His compositions are part of the Great American Songbook, a group of popular songs from musical theater and jazz concerts written by the greatest composers of the early 1900s.

"ORIGINALITY IS THE ONLY THING THAT COUNTS. BUT THE ORIGINATOR USES MATERIAL AND IDEAS THAT OCCUR ROUND HIM AND PASS THROUGH HIM. AND OUT OF HIS EXPERIENCE COMES THE ORIGINAL CREATION."

TIPS FOR YOU!

George said he heard music in the noises around him. He composed some songs while riding a train, and the rhythm of the train can be heard in the music. Spend some time listing to the sounds around you. Can you feel the beat of truck wheels on pavement or in dogs barking? Do you hear music around you like George did?

Ruth Bader Ginsburg

LAWYER, SUPREME COURT JUSTICE

March 15, 1933–

Joan Ruth Bader was born in Brooklyn, New York. She is the second child of Celia and Nathan Bader and was raised in the Jewish faith. Ruth's mother was determined that Ruth would get an excellent education. Her mother died one day before Ruth's high school graduation. Later, Ruth graduated from Cornell University, married Martin Ginsberg, and had two children. She also attended Columbia Law School and graduated first in her class.

Today, Ruth is a U.S. Supreme Court justice, the first Jewish woman to sit on the court. As she rose in her law career to this highest level, Ruth faced discrimination along the way because she was a woman in a mostly male field. Law firms seldom hired women lawyers and when they did, the women were paid less than their male coworkers, and sometimes made to use a side door to enter the building where the law firm had its offices. Ruth was rejected by every law firm she applied to. She worked for a judge for two years, and then went to Sweden to research a book.

In Sweden, Ruth noticed that women and men were more equal than in the United States. She was confronted by this inequality again when she returned to the U.S., took a teaching job at Rutgers University Law School, and was told she would be paid less than the male professors. At Rutgers and later at Columbia Law School, Ruth started publications about gender discrimination and women's inequality.

The Supreme Court makes decisions that strengthen or change the laws of the United States. Ruth's work as a justice is extremely important, as was the work she previously did with the American Civil Liberties Union (ACLU). In the 1970s, she worked as a director of the Women's Rights Project for the ACLU. She brought cases to court to fight against laws that treated women or men unfairly based on their sex or gender. She helped shape today's laws of sexual equality.

"MY MOTHER TOLD ME
TO BE A LADY. AND FOR HER,
THAT MEANT BE YOUR OWN PERSON,
BE INDEPENDENT."

TIPS FOR YOU!

Ruth has a brilliant mind, a just heart, and a fierce personality. She also has a powerful position. Ruth's nickname, RBG, is also the title of a documentary about her. If you watch it, you will see why people say she is indomitable.

Fannie Lou Hamer

CIVIL RIGHTS ACTIVIST

October 6, 1917–March 14, 1977

Fannie Lou Townsend Hamer was born in Montgomery County, Mississippi, the youngest of 20 children. Her family worked as tenant farmers and lived on the plantation where they picked cotton. The plantation owner sold the cotton they picked and kept most of the money. Fannie Lou picked cotton from the age of six. When it wasn't picking season, she learned to read and write in a one-room school. She left school at age 12 to help her parents.

Shortly after the Civil War ended, changes to the U.S. Constitution gave black citizens, including those who had been enslaved, the same rights held by white people. This meant African American men had the right to vote. In 1919, the Nineteenth Amendment gave all women the right to vote. But in the South, state and local governments passed laws to make it difficult for blacks to vote. To register to vote, black people were forced to pass timed, written exercises, called "literacy tests" that were complicated, absurd, and sometimes nonsensical. They were also charged money, and if they hadn't been dissuaded from trying to vote, they were even threatened with violence.

To fight racial discrimination, injustice, inequality, and segregation, African Americans took action and the civil rights movement began. Fannie Lou was one of the movement's brave leaders. She organized black citizens to go to city halls to register to vote, marched in demonstrations, and founded the Mississippi Freedom Democratic Party to give African Americans a voice in politics. She gave a speech to the entire nation at the Democratic National Convention in 1964, and she ran for the U.S. Senate. It was dangerous work that angered many white people. Fannie Lou was fired from her job, shot at by white supremacists, and beaten nearly to death by police. While she survived, other activists were murdered.

The civil rights movement ended Jim Crow laws, which enforced segregation, or separation based on race. It also resulted in the Voting Rights Act of 1965, which finally protected African Americans' right to vote. The Act prohibits state or local laws that prevent blacks from voting. Not only did it take 100 years for all black people to be allowed to exercise the right to vote, it took the efforts—and sometimes blood—of civil rights activists like Fannie Lou.

"NOBODY'S FREE
UNTIL
EVERYBODY'S FREE."

TIPS FOR YOU!

Fannie Lou received many awards for her contributions. In 1993 she was inducted into the National Women's Hall of Fame. You can read more about her and other women who received this honor at www.womenofthehall.org.

DAVID HO

MEDICAL RESEARCHER, DOCTOR

November 3, 1952–

David Da-i Ho was born in Taichung, Taiwan. When David was 12, he and his mother and brother immigrated to the United States. They came to join David's father, who had arrived six years earlier to earn a degree in electrical engineering. Education was very important to the family. After all, it was the reason David's father had been separated from them for so long. David's parents believed that the United States offered many more opportunities to study science and math and to pursue careers.

School in the United States was challenging for David and his brother because they did not understand English. David did well in math, but he struggled with other subjects and worried that his classmates believed he was not very bright. It was uncomfortable for him because he had been a strong student in Taiwan. However, after taking English as a Second Language (ESL) classes and being surrounded by English speakers, David and his brother became fluent and began to excel in school. David graduated with top grades from the California Institute of Technology and then earned a medical degree from Harvard University and the Massachusetts Institute of Technology.

In the early 1980s, David was working as a doctor at a California hospital. He saw an increasing number of people come in with a mysterious illness that doctors and scientists hadn't seen before. We now know that this disease was Acquired Immunodeficiency Syndrome (AIDS), which is caused by the Human Immunodeficiency Virus (HIV).

As David worked with other scientists, he learned more about the virus and how it acted. Then, in 1995, he arrived at some surprising conclusions that would change the way doctors treated the disease. David combined different medications to make a powerful new drug. He gave this new medication to patients not only when the virus was active in their bodies, but when it was hibernating, or inactive, too. David's idea to medicate patients even when the virus seemed weaker worked. His patients improved. Doctors around the world began to treat patients the same way. Though the treatment does not cure a patient of the disease, it allows many to have a better quality of life and to live with the disease longer, sometimes for decades. David is now the founder of a research institute working to develop a vaccine to prevent HIV/AIDS.

"THERE'S ALWAYS HOPE—
THROUGH SCIENCE AND
SCIENTIFIC RESEARCH."

TIPS FOR YOU!

In addition to David Ho, some of
the greatest Americans have been
naturalized citizens. Learn more
about how people become naturalized U.S. citizens: www.uscis.gov.

Billie Holiday

SINGER, VOCALIST

April 7, 1915–July 17, 1959

Billie Holiday was born Eleanora Fagan in Philadelphia, Pennsylvania. Her parents were only teenagers and were unable to take care of a child. Billie went to live with her mother's half-sister in Baltimore, Maryland. At the age of 9, she was sent to a reform school. Her crime? She had stopped attending elementary school. The rest of her childhood was equally stormy. When Billie was 13, her mother took her to New York City, where they survived by finding work wherever possible.

Billie was still a teenager when she found her first singing job at a Harlem nightclub. Though she had not taken music lessons, she had a voice and spirit made for singing jazz and the blues. Her voice was her instrument, and she used it like a musician playing the piano or trumpet. She experimented with a tune, improvising and changing it. Every night she made the same song sound different. She sang with great emotion, as if everything she sang about had happened to her. For 30 years, Billie sang in nightclubs and concert halls filled with people. Her shows at the famous concert venue Carnegie Hall in New York City sold out. She recorded songs she wrote, like "God Bless the Child," and those written by the greatest composers of the times. She turned those songs into classics.

During her career, Billie was the lead singer of several big bands, including those led by Count Basie and Artie Shaw, and she toured the country with them. She was the first full-time African American lead singer to tour the southern United States with a white band leader. She remembered many instances of discrimination during this time, such as being forced to enter through the kitchen instead of the front door because she was black. Later, one of her most famous songs, "Strange Fruit," was about lynching. This was when a mob of white people murdered a person, almost always a black person, and usually by hanging. With songs like these, Billie used her music to protest the violent treatment of African Americans. The subject of the song wasn't new, but using music to challenge people's views about it was. While Billie's music was popular during her lifetime, today she is beloved as one of the greatest jazz singers of all time.

"I HATE STRAIGHT SINGING. I HAVE TO CHANGE A TUNE TO MY OWN WAY OF DOING IT. THAT'S ALL I KNOW."

TIPS FOR YOU!

Listen to a song. Learn the words and tune, so you can sing along with it. Every time you sing it, make it different. Experiment with the tune. Change it. Then you will be improvising just like Billie.

Langston Hughes

JAZZ POET, ACTIVIST

February 1, 1902–May 22, 1967

James Mercer Langston Hughes was born in Joplin, Missouri. Soon after, his father moved to Mexico to escape racism in the United States, and he and his mother moved to Lawrence, Kansas. Langston's mother's relatives were highly educated activists who fought for black people to have the same rights as whites. Langston's grandmother raised him to feel great pride in his race. When she died, Langston and his mother moved to several different midwestern towns. They ultimately settled in Cleveland, Ohio, where Langston went to high school and began to write jazz poetry.

Langston lived in Harlem, New York, during the 1920s and 1930s, when it had more black artists, writers, and musicians than any other place in the world. He became famous for writing about black working people. Some people wanted him to "sugarcoat" what it was like to be black—to make it prettier and taste better. But Langston was honest, and he didn't apologize for it.

Langston used words like they were notes in a song. The rhythm of his poetry reminded black people of how they themselves spoke and moved. His poetry, novels, essays, and newspaper columns were printed in important black-owned publications. Eventually, his writing also appeared in magazines and newspapers owned and read by all races.

Langston expressed the joy and heartache of being black in America. One of his most famous poems is "Harlem." In this piece, Langston asks a question over and over. What happens to a goal or fervent desire that is thwarted or crushed? When your deepest dream is forever out of reach, does it simply disappear, or does it turn to dust, or fester? He asks this question because the dreams of so many black men and women have been "deferred." Today, his poetry is as alive as it was the day he wrote it, and it speaks a truth. His powerful and beautiful jazz poems, novels, and essays continue to be read by children and adults around the world.

"JAZZ, TO ME, IS ONE OF THE INHERENT EXPRESSIONS OF NEGRO LIFE IN AMERICA: THE ETERNAL TOM-TOM BEATING IN THE NEGRO SOUL—THE TOM-TOM OF REVOLT AGAINST WEARINESS IN A WHITE WORLD, A WORLD OF SUBWAY TRAINS, AND WORK, WORK, WORK; THE TOM-TOM OF JOY AND LAUGHTER, AND PAIN SWALLOWED IN A SMILE."

TIPS FOR YOU!

Langston Hughes wrote poetry wherever, whenever, all the time. Be like Langston. Carry a notebook and pen or a tablet everywhere you go and write. You can even take a line from one of his poems and use it to inspire your writing.

Katherine Johnson

MATHEMATICIAN

August 26, 1918–

Katherine Coleman Goble Johnson was born in White Sulphur Springs, West Virginia. Her parents were Joshua and Joylette Coleman, an African American working-class couple who made certain their children were well educated. From her earliest years, Katherine had a knack for numbers. In college, professors noticed she was gifted in math, and one urged her to become a research mathematician. Without knowing exactly what it meant, Katherine knew she wanted to be one.

After graduation, Katherine taught math for a short while and then married and started a family. When she went back to work, she found a job as a "human computer" at the Langley science laboratory. This laboratory later became part of the National Aeronautics and Space Administration (NASA). Before electronic computers were perfected and widely used, people were the computers. African American women were hired to check the male engineers' calculations and ensure they were correct. They were sometimes asked to do the initial calculations. When Katherine was asked to work on a calculation, she did something her coworkers didn't: She asked about the reasons behind the calculations. She insisted on going to meetings with the engineers to learn the background of projects and the need for the calculations. Katherine was already an expert in geometry. When travel to space began, she was perfectly suited to her job.

In 1961, Katherine did the flight trajectory calculations for astronaut Alan Shepard's mission, called Freedom 7. This was the first time an American traveled into space. In 1962, astronaut John Glenn requested Katherine do the calculations for his voyage into space. NASA was beginning to use electronic computers, similar to those we use today, and calculations for John Glenn's space flight had been computed by these new electronic machines. John Glenn refused to start the spacecraft until Katherine signed off on the calculations. Her accurate calculations ensured a safe flight for American astronauts. Katherine retired in 1986 after working at NASA for 33 years.

Katherine has received many awards, including Mathematician of the Year in 1997, and the Presidential Medal of Freedom, awarded to her by President Barack Obama. In 2019, NASA honored Katherine by naming a building for her. It is the Katherine G. Johnson Computational Research Facility at NASA's Langley Research Center in Hampton, Virginia.

"SOME THINGS WILL DROP OUT OF THE PUBLIC EYE AND WILL GO AWAY, BUT THERE WILL ALWAYS BE SCIENCE, ENGINEERING, AND TECHNOLOGY. AND THERE WILL ALWAYS, ALWAYS BE MATHEMATICS."

TIPS FOR YOU!

Do you want to know more about Katherine Johnson and what her years at NASA were like?
Watch the 2016 film *Hidden Figures* or read *Hidden Figures Young Readers' Edition*.

Sal Khan

EDUCATOR, INNOVATOR, ENTREPRENEUR

October 11, 1976–

Salman "Sal" Amin Khan was born in Metairie, Louisiana, near New Orleans. His parents emigrated from India and Bangladesh. Sal attended public schools as a child and later went to the Massachusetts Institute of Technology (MIT), where he earned two bachelor's degrees, one in electrical engineering and computer science and the other in mathematics. He earned a master's degree in business from Harvard Business School and then worked in the field of finance from 2003 to 2009.

Sal is the creator of Khan Academy, a nonprofit organization that offers a free, personalized education online. Students do not earn academic degrees, but they can learn academic subjects, mostly math and science, by using sequential, progressive lessons. The idea for this enterprise was sparked when Sal was asked to tutor a young cousin in math. They did not live near each other, so the tutoring sessions had to be held online. Sal taught his lessons through short videos that he created and uploaded to YouTube. He did not appear on screen in these videos. Instead, he wrote in chalk on a black background. His cousin watched as this writing appeared. The equations grew, were erased, and were replaced by new equations until the lesson was complete. Over time, it became clear that Sal's cousin wasn't the only one watching the videos. Thousands of people were using them to learn.

Sal stopped working in finance and established Khan Academy. His videos are similar to the ones he did for his cousin, but now there are lessons in all levels of math, plus computer programming, economics, physics, chemistry, biology, medicine, finance, art, and history. There are lessons to prepare people for standardized entrance exams for college, law school, and medical school. There is also a free educational app for two- to five-year-olds to help prepare them for kindergarten. Students from more than 190 countries use Sal's videos to learn. His website uses adaptive software. This means students can watch a video tutorial, practice concepts learned in the lessons, and answer questions to assess whether they have learned enough to move forward. If they have learned well, they move on to the next lesson. If not, they continue to practice specific areas they are struggling with. Tens of millions of people use Khan Academy, each learning at his or her own pace, filling in gaps in their knowledge, and then moving forward with new lessons and knowledge.

"I'VE ALWAYS BEEN INTERESTED IN REALLY UNDERSTANDING THINGS. WHEN YOU HAVE A STRONG FOUNDATION, EVERYTHING FALLS INTO PLACE A LOT EASIER LATER ON."

TIPS FOR YOU!

In 2016, PBS aired
"TED Talks: Education Revolution."
This show focused on changes
in education. Look for it at
www.pbs.org/program/ted-talks.

FRED KOREMATSU

CIVIL RIGHTS ACTIVIST

January 30, 1919–March 30, 2005

Fred Toyosaburo Korematsu was born in Oakland, California. His parents were Japanese immigrants who had been in the United States for 14 years. Fred and his three brothers attended public schools and played after-school sports. After graduating from high school, Fred was hired as a welder by a shipyard. He had tried to register for the U.S. Navy but had been denied. After Japan bombed the U.S. Navy at Pearl Harbor in December 1941, Fred was fired from his job at the shipyard because of his Japanese heritage.

Soon after the attack on Pearl Harbor, President Franklin Delano Roosevelt ordered the U.S. military to detain 120,000 Japanese Americans. They were brought to internment camps called relocation centers. Fred was 23 years old when he and his family were notified that they had to report to a relocation center. They were permitted to take only what they could carry. Fred believed the U.S. Constitution protected citizens from this type of discrimination, and he refused to go. He was arrested and locked up in a San Francisco jail. An American Civil Liberties Union (ACLU) lawyer visited Fred and offered to represent him. The case went as high as the U.S. Supreme Court. Lawyers representing the U.S. government argued the government was protecting the country by keeping Japanese Americans in camps. The Supreme Court ruled in favor of the government and against Fred. He was sent to a relocation center and later said conditions at the relocation center were worse than the jail. Eventually, the U.S. Supreme Court made the opposite ruling in another case and the relocation centers were closed.

In 1983, papers were discovered that had been hidden from the Supreme Court. The papers were studies by the FBI and other U.S. intelligence services that found Japanese Americans did not demonstrate higher rates of anti-American thinking or activity than any other group. The ACLU asked that Fred's case be reopened. The Supreme Court erased Fred's criminal record but was unable to overturn the decision. Later, the Civil Liberties Act of 1988 included an official apology to Japanese Americans who were interned during World War II. It also enabled them to receive reparations, which are payments given to people to compensate them, in part, for having been wronged. Fred also received the Presidential Medal of Freedom Award in 1998 from President Bill Clinton.

"EVERY DAY IN SCHOOL, WE SAID THE PLEDGE TO THE FLAG, 'WITH LIBERTY AND JUSTICE FOR ALL,' AND I BELIEVED ALL THAT."

TIPS FOR YOU!

You can learn more about Fred's life and his civil rights work at www.korematsuinstitute.org.

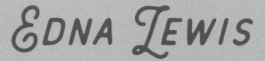

EDNA LEWIS

CHEF, AUTHOR

April 13, 1916–February 13, 2006

Edna Regina Lewis was born in Freetown, Virginia. The town was built and created by formerly enslaved people, including Edna's grandparents. Edna listened to the local's stories and learned from them, including the best way to eat. In Freetown, people knew how to hunt and fish, raise farm animals, forage for plants, and grow crops. They also knew when to capture animals and harvest plants for the best possible flavor. Edna learned from them how to be part of a community where people relied upon each other for survival and celebration. Food was central to their interwoven lives.

As a teenager, Edna moved to New York City. There she went from working as a servant for wealthy families to selling her original hand-sewn clothing to celebrities. She also went from hosting dinner parties for friends to developing a menu and cooking at a friend's new restaurant. Soon she owned the restaurant with him. Edna served up the best Southern cooking in the northern United States. Famous Southern writers who were well acquainted with Southern cooking ate at Edna's restaurant when they visited their New York City publishers. Celebrities like Eleanor Roosevelt, activist and spouse of President Franklin Delano Roosevelt, and Paul Robeson, world-renowned activist and singer, helped make the restaurant famous. Edna went on to publish several cookbooks, beginning with *The Edna Lewis Cookbook*. But it wasn't only her delicious food and brilliant recipes that made Edna a trailblazer. She had a theory, supported by evidence, that black Southern cooking had influenced the dishes most associated with the U.S.

Edna received the James Beard Living Legend Award, perhaps the most prestigious award in the culinary world. She was way ahead of her time because she showed people the best way to eat: local, in season, and homemade. Today, many people follow her philosophy: They buy food from local farmers or grow their own, use ingredients that are in season, and prepare their own meals rather than buying packaged or fast food.

"OVER THE YEARS SINCE I LEFT HOME, I HAVE KEPT THINKING ABOUT THE PEOPLE I GREW UP WITH AND ABOUT OUR WAY OF LIFE. I REALIZE HOW MUCH THE BOND THAT HELD US HAD TO DO WITH FOOD."

TIPS FOR YOU!

Visit the library and look at Edna's book *The Taste of Country Cooking*. It has many stories about Edna's life, and you might find a recipe that you or your family would like to make.

Belva Ann Lockwood

LAWYER, ACTIVIST

October 24, 1830–May 17, 1917

Belva Ann Bennett Lockwood was born in Royalton, New York, the second of six children. Her farming family was very religious and literal in their Christian beliefs. Belva decided to prove religious miracles by acting them out. But when she tried to walk on water, a miracle written about in the bible, she failed. While her attempts did not lead to proof that miracles existed, her willingness to test people's beliefs led to powerful results throughout her life. For instance, even though her father, like most people then, believed women should not go to college, Belva decided that she would.

While at college, Belva attended lectures by a lawyer and became very interested in studying law. At this time, however, women could not become lawyers. It was believed that doing a "man's work" would "unsex" a woman or make her less feminine. Many people thought that women's brains could not handle the stress of practicing law. Despite this, Belva applied to law school. The school rejected her, saying male students would be distracted by female students. Belva didn't give up. She applied to a different law school and was accepted along with several other women. But when Belva finished her studies, the school refused to give her a law degree because it had been criticized for accepting female students. Belva wrote to President Ulysses S. Grant to demand that she be given a diploma. The president did not write back, but soon afterward, the college gave her the diploma. A few days later, Belva was admitted to the bar, which means that she fulfilled the requirements to become a lawyer and could start her career in law.

Even with a law degree, Belva was not allowed to practice law as freely as a man. She had to hire a male lawyer to speak for her in courts where she was not allowed. She would prepare the case herself, then the man would deliver it in court on her behalf. Belva wanted to have access to all courts, including the U.S. Supreme Court. Working alone, Belva successfully lobbied Congress to pass an act allowing female lawyers to appear before the U.S. Supreme Court. Belva then became the first woman to argue a case before the highest court in the United States.

"I LOOK TO SEE WOMEN IN THE UNITED STATES SENATE AND HOUSE OF REPRESENTATIVES. IF [SHE] IS FITTED TO BE PRESIDENT, SHE WILL SOMEDAY OCCUPY THE WHITE HOUSE."

TIPS FOR YOU!

Do you find it hard to believe women did not have the right to vote until 1920? Belva worked for women's right to vote. When will you be old enough to register to vote? Find out at www.usa.gov/register-to-vote.

Thurgood Marshall

LAWYER, U.S. SUPREME COURT JUSTICE

July 2, 1908–January 24, 1993

Thurgood Marshall was born in Baltimore, Maryland, fewer than 50 years after the Civil War ended. During Thurgood's child-hood, Maryland was a segregated state, so people were separated by race. He went to a public school for black children and lived in a nice middle-class neighborhood designated for black people only. His mother was a teacher. His father was a railroad porter and a waiter at an expensive, whites-only club. Mr. Marshall debated current events with his son, teaching him to support his arguments with information from good sources.

Thurgood wanted to attend the University of Maryland School of Law but didn't apply because it did not accept black students. Instead, he went to Howard University, a historically African American school in Washington, D.C. After graduation, he found it difficult to start a private law practice for two reasons: white landlords would not rent an office in downtown Baltimore to a black lawyer and the Great Depression had weakened the economy. Most businesses didn't have money to hire lawyers.

Thurgood began to work for the National Association for the Advancement of Colored People (NAACP) in its Baltimore office and eventually became the organization's chief legal officer. Thurgood and the NAACP fought racial segregation, filing case after case. He started by filing a lawsuit against the University of Maryland, a public school founded by the state of Maryland and subject to federal and state laws. Thurgood argued the state did not offer its black citizens a "separate but equal" public education, which was the law at the time. The court agreed and the law school in Maryland was integrated.

Thurgood is most famous for *Brown v. Board of Education*, a case he argued before the U.S. Supreme Court in 1954. The court ruled that "separate but equal" was unconstitutional and could no longer be used to separate people of different races. Winning this case resulted in the integration of all public schools and changed the course of American history. From 1940 to 1961, Thurgood argued 32 cases before the U.S. Supreme Court and won 29 of them.

In 1967, Thurgood became the first African American member of the U.S. Supreme Court. He served for 23 years. Some of his most important works were the dissents he wrote explaining why he disagreed with the majority decision. These important legal documents can be used in the future to help change laws, ensuring that Thurgood's brilliant legal mind will continue to impact justice in the U.S.

"EQUAL MEANS GETTING
THE SAME THING,
AT THE SAME TIME,
IN THE SAME PLACE."

TIPS FOR YOU!

Go to the U.S. Supreme Court
website to learn more about
the highest court in the land:
www.supremecourthistory.org.

Harvey Milk

GAY RIGHTS ACTIVIST

May 22, 1930–November 27, 1978

Harvey Bernard Milk was born in Long Island, New York. He was the younger son of Jewish immigrants from Lithuania. Harvey was gay, and while there have been places and times in world history when being openly gay was widely accepted, this was not Harvey's experience. In high school and college, Harvey did not tell people that he was gay because he did not want to upset his parents. After Harvey graduated from college, he became a teacher, joined the Navy, and eventually worked on Wall Street, which is New York City's famous financial district.

The 1960s, when Harvey was in his 30s, was a decade of change. Many people were demanding equal rights for women and people of color. Gay people began to fight for equal rights, too. As the country changed, so did Harvey. In 1972, Harvey moved to an area of San Francisco, California, where many gay people lived. At this time, he stopped hiding his sexual orientation and began a career in politics. Harvey wanted to stop the violence against the lesbian, gay, bisexual, and transgender (LGBT) community. He supported policies to protect them from discrimination.

In 1977, Harvey won an election to be on the Board of Supervisors of San Francisco. This made him the first openly gay elected official in California and one of the first in the United States. Harvey became successful right away when a bill he sponsored passed. The bill made it illegal to discriminate against a person due to their sexual orientation when it came to housing, employment, and public places like restaurants and hotels.

Sadly, Harvey and the mayor of San Francisco were shot at city hall by a man who had recently resigned from the Board of Supervisors. The shooter was angry that the mayor would not give him back his position on the board and that Harvey agreed with the mayor's decision.

Harvey was at the forefront of the gay rights movement. He wanted a symbol that would represent the movement and the pride of its people. He asked an artist, Gilbert Baker, to create a symbol that would bring people together and could be carried in marches and parades. Gilbert designed and sewed the rainbow flag that the gay community carries proudly to this day. In 2009, more than 30 years after his death, Harvey was awarded the Presidential Medal of Freedom by President Barack Obama.

"ALL YOUNG PEOPLE, REGARDLESS OF SEXUAL ORIENTATION OR IDENTITY, DESERVE A SAFE AND SUPPORTIVE ENVIRONMENT IN WHICH TO ACHIEVE THEIR FULL POTENTIAL."

TIPS FOR YOU!

Just like Harvey, not every prince wants to date a princess. In the modern fairy tale *Prince & Knight* by Daniel Haack, the prince follows his heart. Daniel also wrote *Maiden & Princess*. You can look for these books at your local library.

John Muir

FOUNDER OF THE SIERRA CLUB, CONSERVATIONIST, WRITER

April 21, 1838–December 24, 1914

John Muir was born in Scotland. At the age of 11, he and his family moved to the United States and lived on a farm in Wisconsin. His father was strict, and John and his brother were expected to work on the farm every minute that there was light in the sky. To help himself wake up and get out of bed on time, John invented a bed that tilted up until he fell out. John treasured his rare free time, and he and his brother often explored the family's acres of fields, enjoying nature.

John went to college for three years but took a job at a carriage parts shop before graduating. An accident at the shop temporarily blinded him. When his vision returned a month later, John had decided to spend as much time in nature as possible. He set out on a 1,000-mile journey from Wisconsin to the Gulf of Mexico. He continued his travels, sailing from Cuba to Panama and up the coast to California. John then trekked to Yosemite Valley in the Sierra Nevada Mountains. While there, he had an idea that the valley had been carved by a glacier during the Ice Age. It was a revolutionary idea, and he was ridiculed for it by scientists. At that time, most scientists believed the valley was created when Earth had crashed in on itself. John's theory is the accepted one today.

John married in 1880. He and his wife had two children, and John began working on his father-in-law's fruit farm. Ten years later, John traveled the world again, experiencing nature. After returning from his travels, John focused on writing. Over his lifetime, he wrote more than 300 articles and 10 books about nature, conservation, and his travels. His books and articles warned people about the devastating effects of sheep and cattle in Yosemite.

In 1890, Congress created Yosemite National Park because of John's efforts. He was also involved with the creation of other national parks, including Grand Canyon National Park and Petrified Forest National Park. John wrote the book *Our National Parks*, which caused President Theodore Roosevelt to visit him. Together, they developed policies to protect the environment. John helped found the Sierra Club in 1892, with the goal of protecting the Sierra Nevada mountain range. This range spans California and Nevada and is the home of Yosemite and other national parks. John was the president of the Sierra Club for 14 years.

"NATURE'S PEACE
WILL FLOW INTO YOU
AS SUNSHINE
FLOWS INTO TREES."

TIPS FOR YOU!

Be like John. Take a walk and observe your surroundings. Are there plants and wildlife that you can see? Bring along a journal to write your thoughts or draw sketches of the world around you.

Edward R. Murrow

JOURNALIST, WAR CORRESPONDENT

April 25, 1908–April 27, 1965

Edward R. Murrow was born Egbert Roscoe Murrow in Polecat Creek, North Carolina. His parents were Quakers, and the family lived on a farm in their Quaker community. Eventually, Edward and his family moved to Washington state in hopes of making a better living. Edward and his two brothers went to public schools. Later, Edward graduated from Washington State College with a major in speech. He decided to change his name from Egbert to Edward.

Edward is credited with inventing American broadcast journalism. This type of journalism started with radio. From the 1920s through the mid-1950s, before most families had televisions, people relied on their radios for the daily news and special reports. Edward was the most famous news journalist of the era. He reported from Great Britain during World War II, introducing his broadcast with the sign-on, "This is London." Americans listened to Edward's firsthand accounts of blazing air battles as he calmly broadcast from the rooftops of London during the Blitz—or the German bombing—of Great Britain. Listeners felt they were up there with him.

Edward and his war reporting moved to France, and then Germany in 1945. When he visited the Buchenwald concentration camp with Allied troops, he reported as he always had. He told his audience the truth about what he was seeing, hearing, and smelling. People were stunned by the horrors he described.

When Edward returned to the United States, he broadcast the radio news show *Hear It Now.* As more American families acquired television sets, he moved his show to television and changed the name to *See It Now.* His show pioneered new techniques in news gathering, filming, editing, and storytelling. These techniques are still used today.

Edward appeared on television for an hour, usually once a week. Each show covered one subject. His goal was to gather the facts and get as close to the truth as he could. Millions of viewers, including important politicians, watched his show. His reports changed history. In his most famous episode of *See It Now,* Edward denounced—or spoke against—the tactics of Senator Joseph McCarthy and his anti-communist campaign. It aired on March 9, 1954.

"WE MUST REMEMBER ALWAYS THAT ACCUSATION IS NOT PROOF AND THAT CONVICTION DEPENDS UPON EVIDENCE AND DUE PROCESS OF LAW."

TIPS FOR YOU!

If you were a journalist on radio or television, how would you sign off? Check out the film
Good Night and Good Luck
which tells Edward's story.

Georgia O'Keeffe

PAINTER

November 15, 1887–March 6, 1986

Georgia Totto O'Keeffe was born on her family's dairy farm in Sun Prairie, Wisconsin, the second of seven children. Here, and later when her family moved to Williamsburg, Virginia, Georgia took art lessons. From an early age, her artistic interest and talent were notable. After high school, she studied at the Art Institute of Chicago in Illinois and then at the Art Students League in New York City.

Georgia began to experiment, creating artwork that was different and original. Most artists created art that looked like objects people could recognize. Georgia made abstract art. She used shapes and lines in her drawings, not to show what an object looked like, but to communicate ideas. Abstract art was new and part of a worldwide art movement called modernism, or modern art. Georgia painted and exhibited her art in New York City, Texas, and New Mexico. When she first visited New Mexico, Georgia was inspired by the area's striking land formations, buildings, and big skies. She returned to New Mexico to draw and paint. Her work there was different from what she had created before. She moved to New Mexico permanently in 1949 and painted there for the next 20 years. She also traveled internationally, creating art in other countries as well.

Georgia overcame challenges to continue her work. She was sometimes ill or exhausted for months at a time and needed to rest. Critics did not always like her artwork and felt that her Southwest images had become too popular. She lost some of her eyesight later in life and needed assistants to help her paint. Despite these obstacles, Georgia spent her life creating art that interpreted the world in a new way. She pioneered a new art movement. Because of this, she has been called the Mother of American Modernism.

"I FOUND I COULD SAY THINGS WITH COLOR AND SHAPES THAT I COULDN'T SAY ANY OTHER WAY— THINGS I HAD NO WORDS FOR."

TIPS FOR YOU!

Georgia's works are in museums around the world. They can be seen in person and online.
The Georgia O'Keeffe Museum is in New Mexico, and you can visit it online at Okeeffemuseum.org.

Susan La Flesche Picotte

DOCTOR, ACTIVIST

June 17, 1865–September 15, 1915

Susan La Flesche Picotte was born on the plains of Nebraska during a buffalo hunt. She was the youngest of four sisters. Their mother was known as One Woman. Their father, Joseph La Flesche, was the last recognized chief of the Native American Omaha Nation. Susan was raised in a section of the Omaha Reservation where families were committed to preserving their traditions while also assimilating into the dominant European American culture.

A sad event in Susan's childhood shaped her life: Susan tried to help a sick woman but instead watched her die. The doctor had been contacted four times, and four times said he would be there soon, but he never arrived. Susan believed that the woman had

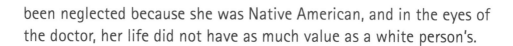

been neglected because she was Native American, and in the eyes of the doctor, her life did not have as much value as a white person's.

Susan's father believed the only way for his tribe and his family to survive was to be educated and understand the European-American culture. He said, "It is either their civilization or extermination." Susan went to a missionary school in Virginia and excelled. She learned three languages in addition to her native tongue. She became a skilled musician. She did not abandon her native culture, but she and her sisters followed her father's advice and helped lead the Omaha Nation into the future.

Susan went to a women's medical school in Pennsylvania and graduated first in her class of 36. She became the first Native American to earn a medical degree. She returned to the Omaha Reservation and was the only doctor, serving more than a thousand people. The Omaha tribe existed between two worlds. For some members, not having the freedom to live as their ancestors had lived crushed their spirit. When Susan returned to the reservation after medical school, alcoholism, cholera, and tuberculosis had devastated the reservation. She struggled to heal her people.

Susan married and moved with her husband to a town near the Omaha Reservation. They had two children. Susan opened a successful private medical practice, but it did not fulfill her dream of opening a private hospital on reservation land. After her husband died, Susan and her children moved back to the reservation and built a house. In 1913, the hospital she'd dreamed of building on reservation land was finished. During her career, Susan cared for her people and also lobbied for better public health and for members of her tribe to receive formal, legal allotments of land.

"THE WHITE PEOPLE HAVE REACHED A HIGH STANDARD OF CIVILIZATION, BUT HOW MANY YEARS HAS IT TAKEN THEM? WE ARE ONLY BEGINNING; SO DO NOT TRY TO PUT US DOWN, BUT HELP US TO CLIMB HIGHER. GIVE US A CHANCE."

TIPS FOR YOU!

To learn more,
visit Nebraskastudies.org
and type *Susan La Flesche Picotte*
into the search bar.

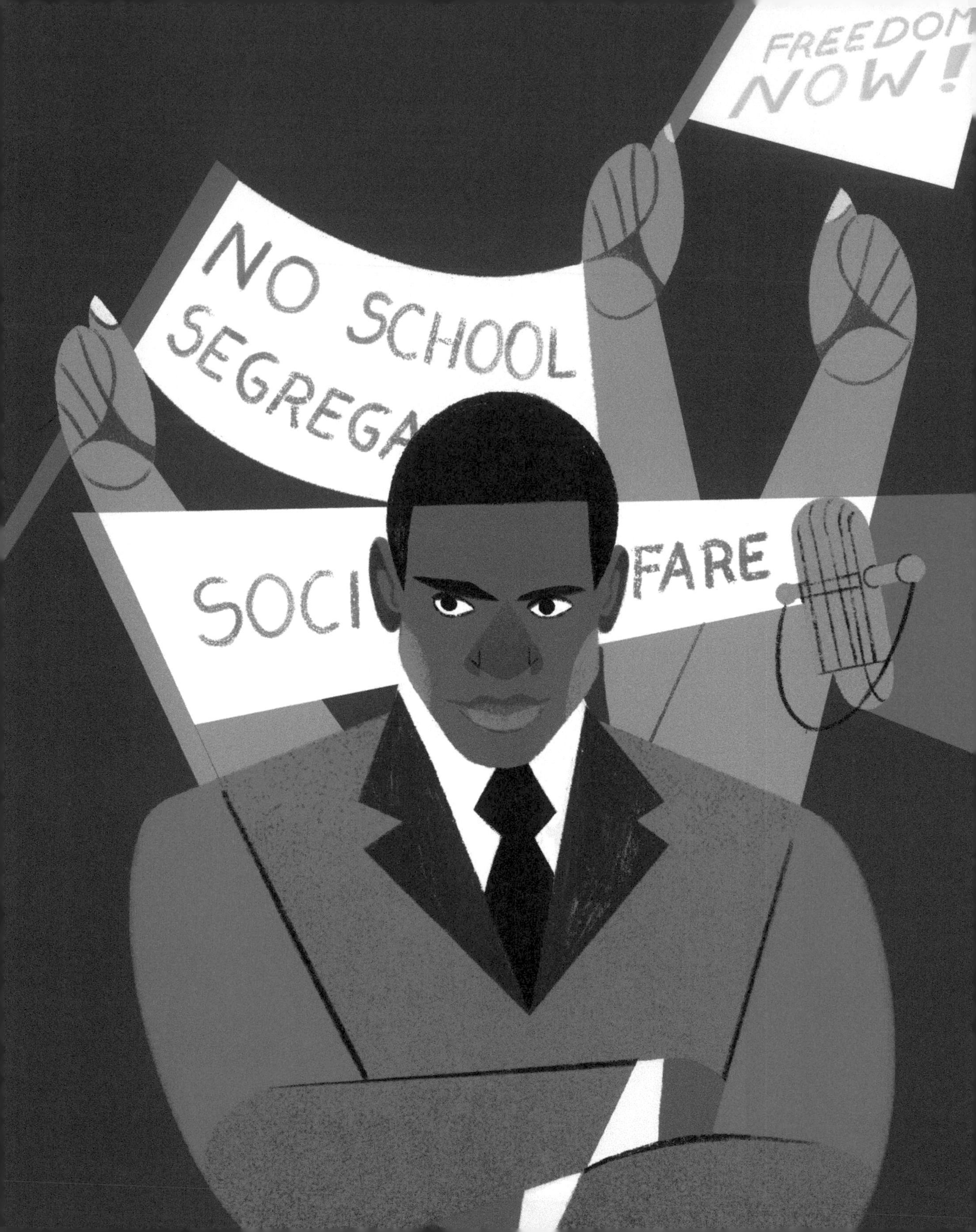
FREEDOM NOW!
NO SCHOOL SEGREGA
SOCI
FARE

Paul Robeson

ACTOR, VOCALIST, ACTIVIST

April 9, 1898–January 23, 1976

Paul Leroy Robeson was born in Princeton, New Jersey. His father had been a slave in North Carolina until he escaped at the age of 15, graduated from a university, and became a minister. His mother, a Quaker teacher whose distinguished family had been in the United States for centuries, was Native American, African, and English. She died when Paul was six, and his father raised the five Robeson children alone.

Paul displayed exceptional intellectual, musical, and athletic gifts from a young age. He received an athletic scholarship to Rutgers University, where he was one of three African American students. Despite facing racial discrimination, he excelled in college and was accepted to Columbia Law School, becoming the only black student in his class. Paul graduated, was admitted to the New York State bar, and joined a law firm. After a white secretary refused to work with him, and the firm's owner admitted clients were afraid a judge would discriminate against them if they had a black lawyer, so Paul would never argue a case in court, he left the field of law.

Paul's wife, an African American scientist, suggested he audition for a local play. This was the beginning of his phenomenal career on stage and screen. His deep baritone voice, superb singing, and impressive acting won over audiences. He was one of the first African Americans to be cast in lead roles, which were usually reserved for white actors. His work spanned a wide range of genres, from Shakespearean plays to modern dramas. Paul was widely respected and critically acclaimed in the United States, but he still encountered racism. At times, he was refused service at a restaurant or jeered by crowds before a performance. As Paul worked and traveled around the world, he experienced less racism in Europe and the Soviet Union than in the United States.

Paul was outspoken about wanting justice for blacks in the United States. After all, his father had escaped slavery, and Paul had relatives living in the South. It was natural that he wanted justice in the United States; the issue was personal for him. But Paul also wanted justice for poor people anywhere in the world. He went to other countries and showed support for political parties, including communist parties, that fought for justice. Paul paid a price for his activism. The U.S. government took away his passport for eight years. More than 50 of his U.S. concerts were canceled. Paul's career was over. While Paul suffered through this period, his legacy is about working to end the suffering of others. He was a powerhouse, who used his immense talent, intellect, and heart to demand justice for workers, the poor, and people of color.

"THE ANSWER TO INJUSTICE IS
NOT TO SILENCE THE CRITIC
BUT TO END THE INJUSTICE."

TIPS FOR YOU!

Listen to the podcast,
"'Ol' Man River':
An American Masterpiece,"
to learn more about Paul Robeson
and hear him sing.

Wilma Rudolph

TRACK AND FIELD ATHLETE

June 23, 1940–November 12, 1994

Wilma Glodean Rudolph was born in Saint Bethlehem, Tennessee. She was the 20th of 22 children. Although her family was poor, her parents, Blanche and Ed, were strong. As Wilma grew, she needed her family's strength. She survived polio, pneumonia, and scarlet fever, but polio paralyzed her leg. Wilma's mother frequently took her on a bus to a medical center 90 miles away to have her leg treated. Family members massaged Wilma's leg four times a day for two years. Wilma had to wear a leg brace and then a special shoe. In secret, she often removed her brace and hopped around on one foot, so she could play like everyone else. She was determined to walk like everyone else, too. Once she was able to walk, she set off running.

Wilma was six feet tall and could sprint as gracefully as a gazelle. When she started competing, she did not win every race, but losing taught Wilma that she needed more than her natural ability to be a champion. She ran longer and longer distances to build her endurance. It worked. At the age of 16, Wilma was the youngest person on the 1956 U.S. Olympic team and won a bronze medal.

Four years later, at the Olympic Games in Rome, Italy, Wilma became the first American woman to win three gold medals in track and field in one Olympics. Like other amateur athletes who participate in the Olympics, Wilma did not earn money for competing. She did earn fame, however. She was invited to the White House, parades were held in her honor, and she received many awards, such as the Associate Press's Female Athlete of the Year award.

Wilma's influence went far beyond sports. She remembered what it was like to grow up in the segregated South, and she wanted to do what she could to promote equality. When her hometown planned a parade to celebrate her performance in the 1960 Olympic Games, she said that she would not participate unless the parade was integrated. They listened to her. There were 40,000 people of all races at the parade.

Wilma retired from running in 1962. Twenty years later, she was inducted into the U.S. Olympic Hall of Fame. She was added to the National Women's Hall of Fame in 1994.

"MY DOCTOR TOLD ME I WOULD NEVER WALK AGAIN. MY MOTHER TOLD ME I WOULD. I BELIEVED MY MOTHER."

TIPS FOR YOU!

Wilma was called the "fastest woman in the world." Before she became a track star, she overcame incredible challenges just to walk. What do you want to achieve? What are the challenges you must overcome to get there?

SACAGAWEA

INTERPRETER, GUIDE

May 1788–December 20, 1812

Sacagawea was born in what is now the state of Idaho. During her lifetime, the area was a colony of Spain, and then of France, and finally became part of the United States. A river ran through the valley where she was born. Her father was the chief of a small Shoshone tribe whose name, Agaidika, means Salmon Eaters. Her family moved often, lived in tepees, and ate the plants they gathered and the animals they hunted. Sacagawea was familiar with these Shoshone lands and waterways.

At the age of 12, Sacagawea was kidnapped while she was with a small group hunting buffalo. Later she was sold to a French-Canadian fur trader to be one of his wives. A few years after that, two explorers, Meriwether Lewis and William Clark, hired the fur trader to be their guide. They said he must bring Sacagawea to be an interpreter on their trip. Lewis and Clark had been sent by President

Thomas Jefferson to map the lands purchased from France in 1803, in what was known as the Louisiana Purchase. These lands were west of the Mississippi River and doubled the size of the United States. Jefferson hoped Lewis and Clark would find rivers connecting the Atlantic Ocean to the Pacific Ocean.

Sacagawea was the only woman on the expedition. She worked for two years without pay, carrying her baby on her back. Lewis and Clark believed Sacagawea, a Shoshone, would be useful in dealing with the Shoshone people who lived in the territory. She was. As they traveled through Shoshone lands, it was the first time many of the native people had ever seen white men. Lewis and Clark also hoped that when natives saw a woman and baby in their group, they would know the expedition was not interested in war. In this way, Sacagawea and her baby protected a group of male foreigners armed with guns.

It was a difficult journey and while Sacagawea did not lead the group, she helped them survive. When their boat nearly capsized and others panicked, she rescued instruments, supplies, and documents. She made decisions about paths to take as they traveled by land. Once, when they met a group of Shoshone and began to trade for horses, Sacagawea recognized their chief. He was her brother. It was a joyful reunion, and her brother provided horses and guides to help them through the Rocky Mountains. She also gathered edible plants to feed the members of the expedition and located medicinal plants to treat them when they were ill. Her intelligence and courage helped make a very dangerous expedition a success.

"I HAVE TRAVELED A LONG WAY WITH YOU TO SEE THE GREAT WATERS (PACIFIC OCEAN) . . ."

TIPS FOR YOU!

The name "Sacagawea" means "Bird Woman" and "Boat Puller." If you could give yourself a name that described you, what would it be?

Arturo Alfonso Schomburg

HISTORIAN, ACTIVIST

January 24, 1874–June 10, 1938

Arturo Alfonso Schomburg was born in Puerto Rico when it was a colony of Spain. His mother was a free black woman from the Virgin Islands. His father was a merchant from Germany. When Arturo was young, the Caribbean Islands were owned and controlled by European nations. The United States was a close neighbor and a powerful nation, and wanted more influence in the area. Arturo and many others wanted Puerto Rico to be independent.

At age 17, Arturo moved to New York City. He went to school and became very involved in social movements. At first, he worked with individuals who wanted Cuba and Puerto Rico to gain independence. But events around the world and in his own life caused Arturo to shift his attention to the black experience in the United States, especially in the South. Arturo began to meet important black figures, like W. E. B. DuBois, a civil rights activist and writer. Arturo read many books written by African Americans and about Africans and African Americans. This interest led him to start the Negro Society for Historical Research.

Arturo gathered a magnificent collection of more than 10 thousand books, artworks, and documents, as well as original letters and manuscripts. All of these materials were related to the history of African people on every continent, and especially African Americans. If anyone suggested that African people and people of African descent had not contributed to the world, Arturo had evidence to prove them wrong. Arturo allowed writers to visit his library to do research, and he shared items with the New York Public Library, which had opened a branch in Harlem. In 1926, Arturo sold his collection to the New York Public Library.

After leaving New York City to help a black university in the South build its own collection of historical documents, Arturo returned to Harlem. He became the curator of his own collection at the New York Public Library. Today it is called the Schomburg Center for Research in Black Culture. It holds more than 11 million items and is a world-renowned research center.

"HISTORY MUST RESTORE WHAT SLAVERY TOOK AWAY."

TIPS FOR YOU!

Arturo loved books.
One way to learn more
about Arturo is to read
Schomburg:
The Man Who Built a Library
by Carole Boston Weatherford.
You may find it at your local library.

Dr. Seuss

AUTHOR

March 2, 1904–September 24, 1991

Theodor Seuss Geisel, or "Dr. Seuss," was born in Springfield, Massachusetts. He was a smart, funny boy who said surprising things. He drew surprising things, too. He especially liked to draw animal cartoons that were inspired by his many visits to the local zoo, where he was sometimes allowed to go "behind the scenes" with his father. Ted's parents encouraged him to be his unique self. At Dartmouth College, Ted was editor-in-chief of the school's humor magazine and he signed his cartoons, "Seuss."

Ted eventually wrote more than sixty famous children's books, but he had other careers as well. First, he tried to be a cartoonist. Eventually, magazines and newspapers began to print his cartoons. Advertising agencies wanted to use them, too, and they paid very well. He became famous for his bug spray ads: "Quick, grab the FLIT!" Despite his success, Ted wanted to create his own stories and fantastical characters. He began to write and draw children's books featuring imaginary beasts, made-up words, and a rhythm that made the words easy for children to remember. Some of his books were made into animated films. Dr. Seuss's success turned into stardom when he published his fourteenth book, *The Cat in the Hat*. It remains one of the most popular children's books of all time and has sold millions of copies in many languages around the world.

Dr. Seuss wrote *The Cat in the Hat* to solve a problem. He believed that the books used to teach children to read were dull. A publisher challenged him to write an exciting book for children with fewer and easier words than he usually used. When he looked at the publisher's list of words, it seemed an impossible task, until he decided to take the first two words that rhymed and work from there. He saw "cat" and "hat," and that was that. *The Cat in the Hat* was revolutionary, unlike any book that had come before, and it changed what children read and how they learned to read.

"ALL OF MY BOOKS ARE
BASED ON TRUTH,
AN EXAGGERATED TRUTH."

TIPS FOR YOU!

Dr. Seuss wanted people to treat each other with kindness. Read a Dr. Seuss book such as *Horton Hears a Who!*, *Yertle the Turtle*, *The Sneetches*, or *The Lorax.* Notice the year that the book was published. Think about what was happening in the world then. Can you figure out the social and political messages that influenced Dr. Seuss as he wrote the story?

Margaret Chase Smith

POLITICIAN

December 14, 1897–May 29, 1995

Margaret Madeline Chase Smith was born in Skowhegan, a small mill town in central Maine. Her mother was a homemaker and her father worked as a barber. Margaret was the eldest of six children. She went to public schools, and after graduating, she became a teacher in a one-room schoolhouse for a short time. Later, while working as a manager for a newspaper, Margaret founded a local chapter of the Business and Professional Women's Club. Margaret married businessman and politician Clyde Smith. In the 1920s, women were expected to stay in the background and support their husbands' careers, and Margaret seemed content to do this.

When Margaret's husband was elected to the U.S. House of Representatives, the two of them traveled from Maine to Washington, D.C. Margaret worked as his secretary. However, Margaret's husband died unexpectedly. In a special election with no challenger, Margaret won and became the first woman from Maine elected to Congress. She served in the U.S. House of Representatives from 1940 to 1949 and the U.S. Senate from 1949 to 1973. She was the first woman in the country to be a member of both the House and the Senate.

Margaret was well known for having integrity. She always did what she thought was right, regardless of what her political party wanted her to do. Although Margaret was a member of the Republican party, she sometimes supported bills sponsored by Democrats and worked alongside them. This bothered some Republicans, who believed that working with Democrats would take power away from their own party.

In 1950, Margaret bravely stood on the Senate floor and gave a speech, "Declaration of Conscience," which catapulted her into the national spotlight. Without ever using his name, Margaret warned Senator Joseph McCarthy to stop accusing individuals of being communists publicly without evidence. He was ruining people's reputations and causing people to lose their jobs, friends, and families. Margaret reminded the senators, and everyone in the country, that the U.S. Constitution and the Bill of Rights give Americans the right to speak freely, assemble with others, protest, and criticize the government. Margaret understood why people were worried about the communist Soviet Union gaining power, but she did not want anyone to trample on Americans' civil liberties. She was the first member of the Senate to denounce the tactics of McCarthy and the House Un-American Activities Committee.

"ONE OF THE BASIC CAUSES FOR ALL THE TROUBLE IN THE WORLD TODAY IS THAT PEOPLE TALK TOO MUCH AND THINK TOO LITTLE."

TIPS FOR YOU!

To learn more about
Margaret's views
and achievements, go to the
Margaret Chase Smith Library online
at Mcslibrary.org.

Dr. Nettie Maria Stevens

GENETICIST, SCIENTIFIC RESEARCHER

July 7, 1861–May 4, 1912

Dr. Nettie Maria Stevens was born in Cavendish, Vermont. After her mother died and her father remarried, he moved the family to Massachusetts. Nettie and her sister received an excellent education at a rigorous private high school. Only one other woman graduated in the years they attended. At that time, it was unusual for a woman to continue her education past high school, but Nettie did so. She worked in education for 13 years as a teacher and librarian, and at the age of 35 traveled to California to attend a new university, called Stanford, where she earned degrees in science. She wrote a scientific paper, which examined infusoria, microscopic creatures living in freshwater.

In Nettie's day, many people believed women had inferior brains. It was legal to discriminate against them. Female scholars were not allowed to attend the best graduate schools, and those who became professors could be forced to give up their jobs if they got married. Despite these challenges, Nettie continued to pursue her higher education. Only one school, Bryn Mawr College, awarded graduate degrees to women. Nettie started her doctorate degree there. Recognized as an exceptional scholar, Nettie was invited to study at zoological institutes in Italy and Germany. When she returned to the United States, Nettie finished her studies and received a Ph.D. in biology from Bryn Mawr and stayed on, first as a research fellow in biology, and later as a research scientist and professor.

In 1905, a scientific foundation gave Nettie money so she could focus on her research. She eventually made a groundbreaking discovery. The question she answered was how do offspring become male or female? Nettie studied beetles to try to answer this question of sex determination. By using a microscope, she was able to see that beetle sperm had chromosomes that were two different sizes. Her research showed that one chromosome was responsible for male offspring and the other for female offspring. These two chromosomes were later named X and Y, which is how they are still referred to today.

Throughout her career, Nettie wrote 38 papers explaining her scientific research. While she was one of the first female scientists to be recognized for her contributions, she did not receive full credit for her important discovery about sex determination because she was a woman. For many years, she was dismissed as "only a lab technician." A male scientist with a similar (but only partially correct) theory was given credit for Nettie's discovery.

"THIS SEEMS TO BE
A CLEAR CASE OF SEX
DETERMINATION."

TIPS FOR YOU!

If your science textbook tells you
that Thomas Morgan made Nettie's
discovery, write to the company and
tell them Nettie did it.

Maria Tallchief

BALLERINA

January 24, 1925–April 11, 2013

Elizabeth Marie Tall Chief was born in the town of Fairfax, in Osage County, Oklahoma. Osage County is a reservation of the Native American Osage Nation. The Osage people became wealthy when oil was discovered on their tribal lands. Maria and her family were financially secure. She was able to take dance and music lessons from the age of three and considered becoming a concert pianist. Maria and her sister continued to study dance seriously in Los Angeles when the family moved to California. At 17, Maria moved to New York City to audition for a ballet company.

Maria was a legendary dancer. She was America's first prima ballerina and one of the best dancers in the world. Her leaps and twirls were filled with passion and energy. Maria danced with the New York City Ballet for 18 years, beginning at the same time the company began in 1947. She danced in starring roles, defining them for future dancers.

The New York City Ballet was co-founded by a choreographer, or dance creator, named George Balanchine. Maria and George were married for six years, and afterward, Maria continued to be George's inspiration. He created 32 ballets for her to dance. She appeared onstage as a dazzling firebird, a sugarplum fairy, and a swan queen.

Maria stopped performing in 1966. After retiring from the stage, she founded a ballet school in Chicago and a ballet company called the Chicago City Ballet. Unfortunately, financial problems caused the company to close in 1987. Maria had a spectacular career as America's foremost ballerina and won many honors. In 1953, the Osage Nation gave her the name Wa-Xthe-Thomba, which means, "Woman of Two Worlds." She was admitted into the National Women's Hall of Fame and presented with a Kennedy Center Honor for her lifetime achievements.

"A BALLERINA TAKES STEPS GIVEN TO HER AND MAKES THEM HER OWN. EACH INDIVIDUAL BRINGS SOMETHING DIFFERENT TO THE SAME ROLE."

TIPS FOR YOU!

You can visit the National Endowment for the Arts online and read about the Nutcracker Ballet, in which Maria danced the lead.

Nikola Tesla

INVENTOR, ENGINEER, PHYSICIST

July 10, 1856–January 7, 1943

Nikola Tesla was born in a mountain village in what is now Croatia. His family was ethnically Serbian. His father was an Eastern Orthodox priest, and his mother was an inventor who came from a long line of inventors. Nikola moved to a city to attend high school, where most classes were taught in German. His math and science education was rigorous. Nikola was grateful to have an inspiring physics teacher who sparked his intense interest in electricity. The teacher, a scientific researcher, built the school's sophisticated laboratory and conducted clever experiments with electricity.

Nikola was a genius. His teachers found his mathematical abilities amazing. He could do advanced calculus in his mind without writing down the complicated equations! He also had a photographic memory and could remember and recite entire books. He could recall objects or pictures he'd seen only briefly and hold images of them in his mind, mentally examining them in tiny detail. Rather than drawing blueprints or constructing models of his inventions in the early stages, as other inventors did, Nikola visualized the invention three-dimensionally. In his mind, he examined it, imagined it working, designed it, tested it, and redesigned it. Nikola has been called a visionary and a futurist. In Nikola's time, many people laughed at his ideas and believed they were impossible. But today many of these ideas have become realities, including smartphones.

Nikola was unable to find investors to pay for his experiments in Europe, so he moved to the United States. He hoped the American inventor Thomas Edison would help him. Edison gave him a job but did not want Nikola to work on his own ideas, but rather focus on Edison's ideas. Nikola quit the job after a disagreement about his payment. A competition developed between the two geniuses, as each improved and perfected his own very different electrical power system. Eventually, the debate was settled. Nikola's method of transmitting power was used to light the world and is the global standard today.

Nikola worked nonstop. He was always thinking of improvements, innovations, and inventions, and he had more than 700 patents. He was the first to invent the induction motor, the Tesla coil, generators, fluorescent lights, the radio, early X-rays, and a remote-controlled boat. He designed an electric power plant that was built at Niagara Falls, which he had dreamed up as a child after seeing only a picture of the waterfalls. You are surrounded by many appliances and electronics that use Nikola's inventions.

"THE MOTORS I BUILT THERE WERE EXACTLY AS I IMAGINED THEM. I MADE NO ATTEMPT TO IMPROVE THE DESIGN, BUT MERELY REPRODUCED THE PICTURES AS THEY APPEARED TO MY VISION AND THE OPERATION WAS ALWAYS AS I EXPECTED."

TIPS FOR YOU!

To learn more about Nikola,
visit the Tesla Science Center online at
Teslasciencecenter.org.

MADAM C. J. WALKER

ENTREPRENEUR, PHILANTHROPIST

December 23, 1867–May 25, 1919

Madam C. J. Walker was born Sarah Breedlove. Her mother gave birth to her on a plantation near Delta, Louisiana, where the family had been enslaved. President Abraham Lincoln had already signed the Emancipation Proclamation at the time of Sarah's birth. That meant that unlike her parents, brothers, and sister, Sarah was born free. Orphaned at a young age, Sarah was unable to attend school because she worked full time as a servant. By age 20, Sarah had married, become a mother, and then a widow. Sarah moved to St. Louis, Missouri, with her daughter and washed laundry for a dollar a day for 18 years. She saved enough money to send her daughter to college.

Sarah was in her late 30s when she started experimenting with chemicals and gels to create a cream that would stop her scalp from flaking and her hair from breaking and falling out. Scalp problems were common at the time because most people didn't have electricity and indoor plumbing and could not bathe frequently. They also shampooed with lye, a chemical that burned the scalp. Sarah developed several hair treatments and began to sell them. After moving to Denver, Colorado, Sarah met and married Charles Joseph Walker. She decided her married name, Madam C. J. Walker, would also be her professional name. She advertised Madam C. J. Walker hair products in newspapers that African Americans read. Within months, she had lots of customers. When she traveled across the country showing black women how to care for their hair with her products, sales rose even more. As Sarah kept improving her business, she opened a factory to make her products and a beauty school to teach hairstylists.

Founded in 1910, the Madam C. J. Walker Manufacturing Company was the top African American business in the country. Walker was the first woman in America to be a self-made millionaire. She made generous donations to organizations benefitting African Americans, and she was a political activist who fought racism. Her hard work made all of her dreams come true: she made a good living, provided her daughter with an education, and built a company that employed thousands of African Americans, mostly women.

"DON'T SIT DOWN
AND WAIT FOR
THE OPPORTUNITIES
TO COME. GET UP
AND MAKE THEM."

TIPS FOR YOU!

There are lots of books about
how to start your own business
even as a child. If you go
to the library, you can look for
Kid Start-Up by Mark Cuban.

IDA B. WELLS-BARNETT

JOURNALIST

July 16, 1862–March 25, 1931

Ida Bell Wells-Barnett was born in Holly Springs, Mississippi, in the middle of the Civil War. She was enslaved until she was three. In the Spring of 1865, the war officially ended, and the Thirteenth Amendment to the U.S. Constitution abolished slavery. Ida and her parents were free. Her parents believed in education, and her father helped found a college, which Ida attended. When her parents and youngest brother suddenly died of yellow fever, Ida became the head of her family at 16. She kept her younger siblings together and started to teach. Eventually, her brothers became carpentry apprentices, and Ida took her sisters to Memphis, Tennessee. She taught school and wrote articles for church newspapers.

Ida wrote about injustice. Her first article described a travel experience she'd had. She had purchased a first-class train ticket and was seated in the ladies' first-class section, when the conductor ordered her to go back to the smoking car with the other black passengers. She refused, saying there was no first-class section there, and the railroad sold her a first-class ticket. The train was stopped, and Ida was removed. She sued the railroad company, and the lower court ruled in her favor and awarded her $500. When her case went to the state supreme court, the ruling was overturned and Ida lost. Ida continued to write about the unfair treatment of minority individuals and groups. She left the field of teaching and became a full-time investigative journalist.

Ida is best known for writing well-researched articles on lynching, a type of murder almost always targeting black men that reached its peak in the late 1800s. She was also famous for leading anti-lynching campaigns throughout her life. Ida began to research and write about this subject when her good friend and his two business partners, who were black, were dragged away and shot by a mob of white men. Ida examined court records, spoke to witnesses, and then wrote a hard-hitting editorial, a kind of newspaper article, that exposed facts about the lynching.

Ida's work angered whites, who rioted. Her newspaper office was ransacked and her life threatened. She was told she would be lynched if she stayed in Memphis. Ida moved to Chicago, where she continued to research lynching in the Southern states, frequently risking her life to do so. In her book, *The Red Record*, Ida shows that lynching was used to remove ambitious blacks and intimidate others. Her activism was instrumental in helping African Americans fight for justice and equality.

"IN SOUTH CAROLINA, IN APRIL 1893, GOV. TILLMAN AIDED THE MOB BY YIELDING UP TO BE KILLED A PRISONER OF THE LAW, WHO HAD VOLUNTARILY PLACED HIMSELF UNDER THE GOVERNOR'S PROTECTION."

TIPS FOR YOU!

Ida believed that shining a light on injustice was the way to stop it from happening. She was brave. Today journalists must also be brave to shine light on injustices. The International Women's Media Foundation (IWMF) shines a light on female investigative journalists. Visit www.iwmf.org to find out why it can take bravery to report the facts.

Anna May Wong

ACTRESS

January 3, 1905–February 3, 1961

Anna May Wong was born Wong Liu Tsong in Los Angeles, California, as a third-generation American. Her parents owned a successful business, but Anna May wanted to be a movie star. She began with very small film roles but was gradually cast in more important parts. Finally, in 1921, she played the lead in *Toll of the Sea*. Anna's father did not approve of her career and made sure the teenager did not leave her dressing room between scenes. Anna May started in silent films. A few years into her career, sound films, called talkies, began. From 1929 on, nearly all films were talkies, and Anna May acted in many of them.

The film industry had rules against interracial couples on screen. This meant that Anna May could not hold hands with or kiss a white actor, even if he was "playing" an Asian character. If the characters in a film were Asian, a white actor and a white actress would wear makeup to appear Asian. Since nearly all leading roles for men were given to white actors, Anna May was not cast in the most important roles that would seem obvious choices for her. Instead, she played stereotypical roles, such as the evil "dragon lady" or the shy "butterfly."

To help her career, Anna May left the United States. In Europe, she was cast in the best roles. She could already speak English and Chinese, and she learned to speak German and French as well. She became a star on both stage and screen and appeared on the covers of magazines all over the world. She socialized with European actors, producers, playwrights, and royalty. When Anna May was offered a contract with a major Hollywood film studio, she returned to California hoping she would be given leading roles, as she was in Europe. She was not, but she accepted the roles she was offered because she wanted to continue to work in film. Fortunately, Anna May was offered more diverse roles in television and on the Broadway stage, and acted regularly. She also narrated a documentary about China for American audiences that importantly introduced European Americans to Asia through a person they felt they knew well.

Anna May was the most successful Asian American actress of her era. Despite her phenomenal career, many Chinese and Chinese Americans were unhappy with Anna May for taking stereotypical film roles, feeling her work reinforced negative views of Asians. Throughout her life, Anna May felt she did not truly belong in either the dominant white culture or in the Chinese American culture. Yet, her celebrity and her work helped bridge the divide between two parts of America, European and Asian, or West and East. And her acting helped pave the way for future Asian Americans in Hollywood.

"IF IT WERE POSSIBLE TO OVERCOME THIS TERRIBLE CENSORSHIP BARRIER, A NEW FIELD WOULD OPEN FOR ME, GIVING ENDLESS CHANCES TO ACT IN GOOD PARTS."

TIPS FOR YOU!

Create a movie-style poster to depict your life with you in the starring role of course. What is the title of the film? What people, real or imaginary, would have roles in your film?

Fanny Bullock Workman

GEOGRAPHER, CARTOGRAPHER, EXPLORER, MOUNTAINEER, TRAVEL WRITER

January 8, 1859–January 22, 1925

Fanny Bullock Workman was born in Worcester, Massachusetts, to a wealthy New England family. Her father was governor of the state, and Fanny was raised as most rich girls at the time were. She was taught at home by governesses and sent to finishing school. After completing school in New York City, Fanny set off for Europe to become more fluent in the foreign languages she had learned in the classroom. Fanny married William Workman, a surgeon who also came from a wealthy New England family, and they had two children.

Fanny and her husband joined adventure clubs that permitted female members. They learned to climb mountains, such as the White Mountains in Maine and New Hampshire. When they moved to Germany, their families paid for them to live well, hire nannies and other staff, and go on travel adventures, some of which took years. Fanny and William left their young daughter and infant son with the hired staff, and off they went. They traveled on a new invention: a bicycle with two wheels of the same size. It worked beautifully. They biked through Europe for thousands of miles and wrote popular travel books.

The pair continued their mountaineering adventures, and Fanny became one of the first women to climb the Matterhorn, a towering mountain between Switzerland and Italy. They rode 14,000 miles through India and Indochina and the longer they rode, the more they felt that the Himalayan Mountains were calling to them. They trekked up the mountains on eight separate trips, creating maps, taking photographs, and writing about the geography for scientists and fellow climbers to use in the future. Their books were filled with descriptions of how local women were treated everywhere they went.

This was the Victorian age, and Fanny was unconventional because she did not stay home and take care of her children and husband. At a time when climbing the Himalayas was considered an activity only for men, Fanny set multiple women's altitude records. This means that she climbed higher than any other American or European woman ever had. The highest altitude she reached was over 26,000 feet. She also gave lectures at the most prestigious universities and exploration clubs in Europe and received many academic honors for her explorations and writing. Fanny proved to the world that women could jettison, or cut loose, their petticoats, and handle the rigors of climbing the highest mountains.

"... IT BEHOOVES WOMEN,
FOR THE BENEFIT OF THEIR SEX,
TO PUT WHAT THEY DO ...
ON RECORD."

TIPS FOR YOU!

Before anyone ever breaks records in any field, including exploration, he or she sets goals. Write your goals, and then list the steps it will take to reach each one. You can do it!

Babe Didrikson Zaharias

OLYMPIC GOLD MEDALIST IN TRACK AND FIELD, PROFESSIONAL GOLFER, CO-FOUNDER OF THE LADIES PROFESSIONAL GOLF ASSOCIATION

June 26, 1911—September 27, 1956

Babe Didrikson Zaharias was born Mildred Ella Didrikson in Port Arthur, Texas. Her parents, Hannah Marie and Ole, had emigrated from Norway. Babe was the sixth of seven children. Her father, a carpenter, wanted his children to have a lot of physical exercise. Her mother had excelled at winter sports in Norway. Mildred played and competed with her brothers from the time she could first walk. As she grew, her interest in sports stayed strong. She earned her nickname, "Babe," after she hit an amazing number of home runs in one baseball game, just like the great Babe Ruth.

Babe didn't limit herself to playing only one sport. In high school, she was unstoppable in volleyball, baseball, tennis, and swimming. She also excelled in basketball and led her team to win the national championships three years in a row. Then she focused on track and field. Just two years after seeing her first track and field meet, Babe was winning gold and silver medals at the 1932 Olympic Games in Los Angeles, California, where she threw a javelin 143 feet to break the world record. She broke her own world record for the 80-meter hurdle and placed second in the high jump. During the Olympics, she was invited to play golf and was introduced to it for the first time. The next year, she began to play golf seriously. Golf brought Babe even greater fame. She won amateur tournaments in the U.S. and abroad, and turned professional, playing her first pro tournament in 1948. She won 82 golf tournaments throughout her career, including three U.S. Women's Opens.

The Associated Press awarded her the Female Athlete of the Year six times. She was also named Woman Athlete of the Half Century in 1950. Many people believed she was the greatest U.S. female athlete of all time. One famous sportscaster of the day went further, saying Babe was the greatest U.S. athlete, female or male. Babe changed women's sports, most notably, women's golf. She co-founded the Ladies Professional Golf Association with 12 other women golfers. It has provided opportunities for female golfers for more than 70 years.

"MY PHILOSOPHY?
PRACTICE, PRACTICE,
PRACTICE—AND WIN."

TIPS FOR YOU!

Babe was an international star in sports at a time when women were expected to stay home and take care of a husband. Who do you think the best female athletes are today? Do you think they are treated differently than male athletes?

HOWARD ZINN

ACTIVIST, HISTORIAN, PLAYWRIGHT

August 24, 1922–January 27, 2010

Howard Zinn was born in a working-class neighborhood in Brooklyn, New York. His parents were Jewish immigrants. Howard flew bombing missions during World War II, including dropping napalm on German troops. His experiences in the military profoundly influenced his point of view. He became a dedicated antiwar activist, protesting U.S. military activities in Central America and the U.S. wars in Afghanistan and Iraq.

Howard was a professor, writer, and historian. He investigated past events, digging for facts that weren't in history textbooks. He believed that children were taught fairy tales—stories that showed the United States in the best possible light and left out difficult truths. While it is common for governments to want their citizens to feel loyal to the nation, Howard felt it was also important for students to understand that history can be viewed from different perspectives. Howard set out to learn more about United States history and to present it in what he believed was a more honest way. His readers should remember that he, too, had a perspective. He promoted a leftist political view of social and economic justice. And he was adamantly opposed to war.

Howard was an adult when he learned about a coal miners' strike in Colorado in 1914. The strike led to the deaths of 75 miners, women, children, and National Guard troops. Howard wondered why this important event, called the Ludlow Massacre, had been left out of the history books. He wrote many articles about it, which brought the tragedy to public attention. It is now taught in high school and college classes.

Howard also wrote 20 books filled with facts about the past that were not usually included in history textbooks. His most important work, *A People's History of the United States: 1492 to the Present*, has sold two million copies. In this book, Howard tells the story of the United States from the perspective of ordinary people—tenant farmers, factory workers, union organizers, Native Americans, African Americans, and others whose voices were not heard before. In 2009, a year before Howard's death, a documentary based on his work was released. It is titled *The People Speak.*

"WE DON'T HAVE TO ENGAGE IN GRAND, HEROIC ACTIONS TO PARTICIPATE IN THE PROCESS OF CHANGE. SMALL ACTS, WHEN MULTIPLIED BY MILLIONS OF PEOPLE, CAN TRANSFORM THE WORLD."

TIPS FOR YOU!

Howard was passionate about certain political issues and made his opinions known to people around him by writing, giving speeches, lobbying for change, and protesting. Is there an issue that moves you? Whatever it is you care about, design a sign. Think of a short slogan or phrase that explains your point of view. Hang your sign on a wall.

ZITKÁLA-ŠÁ ("RED BIRD")

WRITER, ACTIVIST

February 22, 1876–January 26, 1938

Zitkála-Šá was born on the Yankton Indian Reservation in South Dakota. Her name at birth was Gertrude Simmons, which she eventually changed to Zitkála-Šá. Zitkála-Šá means Red Bird. Zitkála-Šá and her siblings were raised by their mother, a member of the Dakota tribe, whose name was Reaches for the Wind. Her father was Felker Simmons, a German American, who left the family when Zitkála-Šá was very young.

Until she was eight years old, Zitkála-Šá lived on the reservation, learned Native American ways, and was happy. Then Christian missionaries took her and other children away to a school in Indiana to practice another religion, Christianity, and learn a different language, English. She also studied how to be a servant. Zitkála-Šá loved learning to read and write and to play musical instruments. However, she hated being forced to learn housekeeping, pray to the Christian God, and give up her Native American ways. She also missed her mother and her tribe.

Zitkála-Šá stayed at the school for four years and then went back to the reservation and her family. She struggled for the next four years because she felt she no longer belonged there. Her mother wanted her to stay with the family, but Zitkála-Šá made the decision to return to school. At school, she did so well that she was offered a scholarship and attended Earlham College in Indiana. She was offered another scholarship and studied violin at the New England Conservatory of Music in Boston. Even then, she did not feel comfortable in either Native American or European American culture.

Zitkála-Šá is famous for her writing and her activism. Her books were popular and her articles were published by the most respected magazines of the day, *Atlantic Monthly* and *Harper's Monthly*. Her writing preserved Native American stories from many tribes. She also wrote about her life before she was educated by the missionaries and as an older child and young adult feeling torn between tribal tradition and assimilation, which means accepting and fitting into another culture.

As an activist, Zitkála-Šá worked to expand the rights of Native Americans. She pushed for Native Americans to have good health care, better education, and the right to vote. She helped create and pass important laws, including the Indian Citizenship Act of 1924 and the Indian Reorganization Act of 1934.

"LIKE A SLENDER TREE,
I HAD BEEN UPROOTED
FROM MY MOTHER,
NATURE, AND
THE GREAT SPIRIT."

TIPS FOR YOU!

Zitkála-Šá wrote
The School Days of an Indian Girl
about her life as a child.
Look for it online or at
your local library.

More Inspiring People to Explore

ROBERT SENGSTACKE ABBOTT (1870–1940) was an African American lawyer, newspaper publisher, and editor. Abbott founded *The Chicago Defender* in 1905 with 25 cents. It became one of the most important African American newspapers in the United States.

ALVIN AILEY (1931–1989) was an African American dancer and choreographer who founded his own dance company in 1958 with eight black dancers. The Alvin Ailey American Dance Theater continues to be a popular and respected company 60 years later.

CESAR CHÁVEZ (1927–1993) and his wife, Helen (Fabela) Chávez, founded the National Farm Workers Association, which later became the United Farm Workers of America (UFW). It is the nation's largest union for farm laborers. It actively works for laws and reforms related to pesticides, immigration, and worker protections.

DUKE ELLINGTON (1899–1974) was one of the most influential jazz composers. His instrumentals have become jazz classics, and he was a band leader for nearly 50 years.

JUAN FELIPE HERRERA (1948–) was chosen to be the official poet of the United States, serving as the first Latino U.S. Poet Laureate from 2015 to 2017. His duties included encouraging people in the U.S. to read and write poetry. In addition to being a poet, he is a performer, writer, cartoonist, and teacher.

EDWARD HOPPER (1882–1967) painted the rocky coast of Maine and the architecture of Manhattan in the style of modern realism. His city scenes explored the spaces in between its inhabitants, expressing solitude and loneliness. His most famous painting is *Nighthawks*.

RUTH BANCROFT LAW (1887–1970) was an aviation pioneer. She broke air speed and altitude records. She also tried to persuade the U.S. Air Force to allow women to fly military aircraft in World War II. To learn more about her, visit the Smithsonian National Air and Space Museum's Women in Aviation and Space History website.

MAYA YING LIN (1959–) is a landscape architect and artist. She is best known for designing the Vietnam Veterans Memorial in Washington, D.C., while she was still a college student. You can visit her website at www.mayalin.com.

MARGARET MEAD (1901–1978) was the most famous anthropologist in the world during the 1960s and 1970s. She traveled through the South Pacific and became an expert on the influence of cultural conditioning on child-rearing and gender roles. She wrote 23 books.

SELENA QUINTANILLA (1971–1995) was a beloved Mexican American singer and songwriter. Her phenomenal success moved Texan-Mexican folk music known as Tejano music into the mainstream music industry.

DALIP SINGH SAUND (1899–1973) was born and raised in India, where he attended boarding schools, and then immigrated to the United States. After he gained citizenship in 1949, he became the first Asian American to be elected to a national office. He served in the House of Representatives for six years.

SHEL SILVERSTEIN (1930–1999) wrote the famous children's books *Where the Sidewalk Ends, A Light in the Attic,* and *The Giving Tree.* He was also a cartoonist, songwriter, playwright, and poet. You can learn more about Shel Silverstein at www.shelsilverstein.com.

JIM THORPE (1888–1953) has been called the greatest athlete of the 20th century. Before playing baseball and football professionally, Jim won two gold medals at the 1912 Olympic Games in Stockholm, Sweden. He was the first Native American to win Olympic gold. There are many books about Jim Thorpe. An especially good one is *Jim & Me* by Dan Gutman.

ANDY WARHOL (1928–1987) was a pioneering artist in the pop art movement. His work includes painting, silk screening, sculpture, film, and photography. His *Campbell's Soup Cans* (1962) is a classic piece of his art recognized by most adults. To learn more about Andy Warhol and other influential artists, visit the Tate Museum online at www.tate.org.uk.

DANIEL HALE WILLIAMS (1856–1931) was an African American surgeon who was the first in the United States to perform a successful heart surgery to repair a wound. He also founded Provident Hospital in Chicago, Illinois. It was the first hospital in the United States to provide medical training for black doctors and nurses.

ABOUT THE AUTHOR

LISA TRUSIANI is a storyteller, and one of her favorite subjects is people. She writes about characters she's created in her imagination, and she writes about real people, living and dead. She loves to research life in the past and often imagines going back in time to meet trailblazers and other fascinating people. Lisa has written award-winning comic book stories for Marvel Entertainment and a syndicated newspaper strip, "Apt. 3-G," for King Features. She is happiest writing when she is writing for children and teens. Lisa lives in Maine where she grew up and then graduated from Bowdoin College. She and her graphic-novelist husband, Rick Parker, have two sons who are smart, funny, and kind.

CPSIA information can be obtained
at www.ICGtesting.com
Printed in the USA
JSHW010754211119
2573JS00001B/1